HITLER'S WAR MACHINE

GERMAN ARTILLERY IN COMBAT

EDITED AND INTRODUCED BY BOB CARRUTHERS

Pen & Sword
MILITARY

This edition published in 2013 by
Pen & Sword Military
An imprint of
Pen & Sword Books Ltd
47 Church Street
Barnsley
South Yorkshire
S70 2AS

First published in Great Britain in 2012 in digital format by
Coda Books Ltd.

Copyright © Coda Books Ltd, 2012
Published under licence by Pen & Sword Books Ltd.

ISBN 978 1 78159 133 8

A CIP catalogue record for this book is
available from the British Library.

All rights reserved. No part of this book may be reproduced or transmitted in any form or by any means, electronic or mechanical including photocopying, recording or by any information storage and retrieval system, without permission from the Publisher in writing.

Printed and bound by
CPI Group (UK) Ltd, Croydon, CR0 4YY

Pen & Sword Books Ltd incorporates the Imprints of Pen & Sword Aviation, Pen & Sword Family History, Pen & Sword Maritime, Pen & Sword Military, Pen & Sword Discovery, Pen & Sword Politics, Pen & Sword Atlas, Pen & Sword Archaeology, Wharncliffe Local History, Wharncliffe True Crime, Wharncliffe Transport, Pen & Sword Select, Pen & Sword Military Classics, Leo Cooper, The Praetorian Press, Claymore Press, Remember When, Seaforth Publishing and Frontline Publishing

For a complete list of Pen & Sword titles please contact
PEN & SWORD BOOKS LIMITED
47 Church Street, Barnsley, South Yorkshire, S70 2AS, England
E-mail: enquiries@pen-and-sword.co.uk
Website: www.pen-and-sword.co.uk

CONTENTS

Introduction 5

Enemy Self-Propelled Guns—A Summary of
Known Equipment 7

German Self-Propelled 150-mm Howitzer 16

New Axis Self-Propelled Guns 18

New Self-Propelled Gun 19

Notes on German Divisional Artillery 23

Observations on German Artillery Tactics 28

Deceptive German Artillery Methods 29

Notes on German Artillery Forward Observers 31

German Antiaircraft Artillery 34
    SECTION I. ORGANIZATION 34
    SECTION II. WEAPONS AND EQUIPMENT 42
    SECTION III. USE OF AA WITH FIELD FORCES 77
    SECTION IV. USE OF AA IN DEFENSE OF
    GERMANY AND REAR AREAS 92
    SECTION V. CONCLUSIONS 111

Artillery with a German Tank Division 113

German Visual Signal System for Artillery
Fire Control 116

75-mm Assault Artillery 118

Artillery in the Desert 123
    SECTION I. ORGANISATION 124
    SECTION II. EQUIPMENT 126
    SECTION III. TACTICS 140

New German Heavy Artillery 171

New German 105-mm Gun-Howitzer 174

The Employment of Field Artillery 176

Artillery Command in the German Army 179

Ruses for Concealing Artillery Positions 182

Employment of German Antiaircraft Artillery at Sevastopol 184

Artillery in Combat in Wooded Areas 186

Six-Barrel Rocket Weapon (The Nebelwerfer 41) 193

Tactical Employment of German 75-mm Assault Gun 199

INTRODUCTION

This book forms part of the series entitled 'Hitler's War Machine'. The aim is to provide the reader with a varied range of materials drawn from original writings covering the strategic, operational and tactical aspects of Hitler's army. The concept behind the series is to provide the well-read and knowledgeable reader with an interesting compilation of related primary sources which together build a picture of a particular aspect of World War II.

I am pleased to report that the series has been well received and it is a pleasure to be able to bring original primary sources to the attention of an interested readership. I particularly enjoy discovering new primary sources, and I am pleased to be able to present them unadorned and unvarnished to a sophisticated audience. The sources speak for themselves and the readership I strive to serve is the increasingly well informed community of reader/historians which needs no editorial lead and can draw its own conclusions. I am well aware that our community is constantly striving to discover new nuggets of information, and I trust that with this volume I have managed to stimulate fresh enthusiasm and that some of these articles will provoke readers to research further down these lines of investigation, and perhaps cause established views to be challenged once more. I am aware at all times in compiling these materials that our relentless pursuit of more and better historical information is at the core our common passion. I trust that this selection will contribute to that search and will help all of us to better comprehend and understand the bewildering events of the last century.

This volume is comprised of information and documents on the vast array of German artillery pieces, and the men who operated them, from the difficulties of warfare in problematic terrain such as desert and forest, the tactics used by the men on the ground, to the facts and figures of the weapons themselves.

In order to produce an interesting compilation giving a flavour of events at the tactical level I have returned once more to the US Intelligence series of pamphlets, which contain an intriguing series of contemporary articles on weapons and tactics. I find this series of pamphlets particularly fascinating as they are written in the present tense and, as such, provide us with a sense of what was happening at the face of battle as events unfolded.

Thank you very much for buying this volume, I hope you find something new and interesting in these pages and I sincerely hope it earns its place in your library.

Bob Carruthers
Edinburgh 2012.

ENEMY SELF-PROPELLED GUNS - A SUMMARY OF KNOWN EQUIPMENT

Tactical and Technical Trends, No. 25, May 20, 1943.

a. General

Self-propelled guns represent one of the technical advances made in ordnance during this war. The following account, from British sources, of German equipment shows the considerable interest which this development has aroused. Several descriptions and sketches of these guns have already been published in earlier issues of Tactical and Technical Trends.

With reference to German self-propelled guns the following general points are worthy of note:
- There are no known German self-propelled heavy antiaircraft guns;
- With regard to antitank guns, while there have been many local improvisations, the present German tendency is to provide self-propelled mounts for the heavier antitank weapons only;
- In every case standard guns and standard chassis, whether semi- or full-tracked, are used;
- All self-propelled guns are provided with AP and HE ammunition, and can thus effectively engage both "soft" and armored targets.

b. German AA/AT Guns

(1) 20-mm AA AT Gun

Although primarily an antiaircraft gun, this piece can also be used against tanks. Mounted on a 1-ton half-track (see figure 1) with a gasoline engine, it usually tows a single-axle ammunition trailer. The armament is a long, thin-barreled, 20-mm, high-velocity gun. The weight in action is 4.5 tons; the length, 15 ft. 7 in., the width,

Fig. 1

7 ft. 1 in. and the height, 6 ft. 7 in. On roads, the radius of action is about 137 miles; cross country, about 93. The crew is seven men.

There are two versions of the gun itself, namely the 20-mm Flak 30 and the 20-mm Flak 38. The gun, mounted in front, may or may not be shielded. It fires 20-mm, .260-pound, high-explosive shells at a high muzzle velocity of 2,950 f/s, the .327-pound AP shell at 2,625 f/s, and the .223-pound AP 40 shot at 3,270 f/s. The firing rate is 120 rpm. The horizontal range is 5,320 yards. The mount gives an all-around traverse and an elevation varying from minus 12 degrees to plus 90. At 400 yards, the AP shell will pierce .98 inch of homogenous armor at an impact angle of 30 degrees, and 1.50 inches at normal. At 400 yards' range, the AP 40 shot will pierce 1.46 inches at 30 degrees, and 1.69 inches at normal.

(2) 20-mm Four-Barreled AA/AT Gun

This is a Vierling (quadruple) gun on an 8-ton half-track (see Tactical and Technical Trends, No. 4, p. 4) 22 ft. 6 in. long by 7 ft. 11 in. wide and 10 ft. 10 in. high, weighing, ready for action, 11.5 tons. The gasoline engine develops 140 brake horse power, giving a radius of action on the road of 155 miles, and about 62 cross country. The crew is probably eight. The armament is "a quadruple 20-mm Flak 38, with an all-around traverse and an elevation stated as from "minus 10 to plus 100" (apparently 10 degrees past vertical--which seems odd, but may be useful when firing at planes passing directly overhead). The range, penetration, and ammunition are substantially the same as for the Flak 30 and 38 previously noted.

(3) 37-mm AA/AT Gun

While like the 20-mm primarily an antiaircraft gun, this 37-mm gun can be used for horizontal fire. It may be identified by the

FIG. 2

long, slender barrel with a conical muzzle brake (see figure 2), and it usually tows an ammunition trailer. The mount is a 5-ton, half-tracked vehicle, with a 130-HP gasoline motor giving a 156-mile radius on the road, and about 62 miles cross country (which seems rather small). The length and breadth are 20 ft. 7 in. by 7 ft. 6 in.; the height is 9 ft. 2 in. The crew is eight men.

Like the 20-mm, the 37-mm Flak 36 is a high-velocity gun, delivering an HE shell at 2,690 f/s at the muzzle. The horizontal range is slightly over 7,000 yards, and the rate of fire, 60 rpm. There is all-around traverse, and an elevation of from minus 5 to plus 85 degrees.

(4) 50-mm Self-Propelled AA/AT Gun

This weapon, the 5-cm Flak 41, is known to exist, but details are lacking. Presumably, it may be a development of the standard 50-mm antitank gun (5-cm Pak 38) described in Tactical and Technical Trends, No. 15, p. 38, which gives a reported muzzle velocity of 3,940 f/s to an AP shot of 2.025 pounds, and 2,740 f/s to a 4 lb. 9 oz. AP tracer shell.

(5) 88-mm Self-Propelled Multi-Purpose Gun

A self-propelled version of the "88," the 8.8-cm Flak 36 Sfl, is known to exist. At one time the gun was said to be mounted on a 12-ton half-track, but this mounting is believed to have been unsatisfactory. Various other mounts have been reported, the most likely of which is the PzKw 4 (medium tank) chassis. In this case, the gun probably has a limited traverse and cannot deliver antiaircraft fire. It fires a 20-pound HE shell, or a 21-pound AP, with an armor-piercing cap surmounted by a "wind splitter" ballistic cap. At 500 yards the projectile will penetrate 4.33 inches of armor at a 30-degree angle, and 5.07 inches at normal. When the range is lengthened to 1,000 yards, penetration falls to 3.30 and 3.93 inches, respectively. The maximum horizontal range is 16,200 yards, but the sight is graduated to 10,340 yards only. The practical rate of fire is from 15 to 20 rpm. The number in the crew is not stated.

c. German Self-Propelled Antitank Guns

(1) 28-mm AT Gun, Model 41

It may be that this gun is a local improvisation. Firing forward, it is mounted on a light half-track, with a coffin-shaped, armored body. The small weapon may be identified by its prominent muzzle brake and flat, double shield. The chassis is that of a 1-ton half-tracked vehicle. The battle weight is about 6 tons. The dimensions are 15 ft. 6 in. by 6 ft. by 7 ft.; the motor is a 100-hp gasoline engine. Cross country, the radius of action is about 75 miles; on the road, 120. Varying from about .39 inch on the front, the light armor is .32 inch elsewhere. The crew is believed to number five.

The ultra-modern, high-velocity gun is the 2.8-cm (1.1 in) Pz.B. 41. It is choke-bored from 28 mm at the breech to 20 (.79 in) at the muzzle, and has a muzzle velocity of 4,580 f/s. At 100 yards it will drive a .287-pound shot through 2.72 inches of armor at 30 degrees, and through 3.31 inches at normal angle. At 100 yards the penetrations are 2.09 and 2.56 inches, respectively. The traverse is 90 degrees, the elevation from minus 5 to plus 45.

(2) 37-mm AT Gun

Like the 28-mm, this gun may be a local improvisation. The obsolete 37-mm antitank gun, with or without a shield, fires towards the front and is mounted on a 3-ton armored half-track; weight in

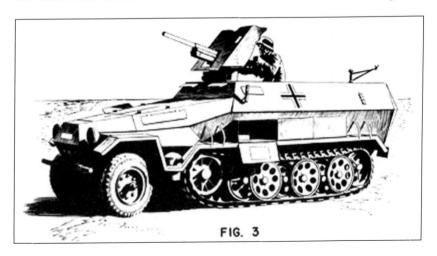

FIG. 3

action is 8.4 tons (see figure 3). The dimensions are: length 18 ft. 8 in., width 6 ft. 10 in., height about 7 ft. 6 in. The gasoline motor develops 100 hp. On the road, the radius is 187 miles, and 81 across country. In front, the armor is from .39 inch to .59 inch in thickness, and on the sides, .32 inch. The crew numbers three.

This gun has a muzzle velocity of 2,500 f/s for the 1.68-pound AP shell and 3,380 (estimated) for the .786-pound AP 40. The HE weighs 1.38 pounds. At 200 yards, the AP shell will penetrate 1.65 inches at 30 degrees and 2.20 inches at normal angle; at 600 yards, 1.34 and 1.81 inches, respectively. The AP 40 at 100 yards pierces 2.68 inches at 30 degrees and 3.11 inches, normal; but with the light AP 40 shot, at 400 yards, the penetration falls to 1.93 and 2.28 inches. The effective range is 600 yards. The maximum traverse is 60 degrees, and the elevation varies from minus 8 to plus 25 degrees.

(3) 47-mm AT Gun

This piece of equipment is the Czech antitank gun mounted in a three-sided shield on the turretless chassis of the PzKw 1 Model B tank. It may be recognized by the five bogie wheels (of which the rear four are partially obscured by a girder), a front sprocket, a rear idler, and four return rollers. The gun-shield is open at the back and top. The gun is fitted with a muzzle brake, and the recuperator is above the barrel. The weight is 7.5 tons; the dimensions 13 ft. 7 in., 6 ft. 7 in., and 7 ft. A 100-hp gasoline engine will drive the vehicle on a radius of action of 70 miles cross country and 90 on the road. The crew is three.

The Skoda gun has a 30-degree traverse with an elevation of from minus 8 degrees to plus 12. The AP tracer shell, 3.68 pounds, has a velocity of 2,540 f/s, penetrating at 300 yards 2.32 inches of armor at 30 degrees, and 2.99 inches at normal angle. At 1,000 yards the respective penetrations are 1.85 and 2.44 inches. An HE shell of 5.07 pounds and an AP 40 shot of 1.81 pounds are used. The effective range is not stated, but is apparently 1,000 yards. About 74 rounds are carried.

(4) 50-mm AT Gun

The only evidence of this equipment is a photograph, which showed a long-barreled gun in a fixed, square turret on an armored half-tracked vehicle of unconventional design. There is a large muzzle brake at the end of the gun, which is believed to be the standard 50-mm Pak 38.

(5) 75-mm AT Gun, on a PzKw 38(t) Chassis

This equipment consists of the 75-mm (2.95-in) antitank gun (Pak 40) mounted on the turretless chassis of the light Czech PzKw 38(t). The suspension consists of four large Christie-type bogie wheels, two return rollers (mounted above the space between bogie wheels 1 and 2, and 2 and 3, respectively), a front sprocket, and a rear idler. In action, the weight is 10 tons. The dimensions are 15 ft. 3 in. by 7 ft. by 7 ft. 2 in. A 125-hp gasoline motor gives a radius of 143 miles on the road, 103 cross country. A plate of .98-inch armor with, possibly, an additional plate of the same thickness riveted on, protects the front. The sides are 1.18 inches toward the front, and .59 inch toward the rear of the sides and the back of the hull. The crew is probably four.

The gun is a 75-mm antitank piece, thought to have a performance similar to the 75-mm long-barreled tank gun mounted in the latest PzKw 4's. This latter gun has the moderate velocity of 2,400 f/s, giving a penetration (presumably with a 15-pound, capped AP projectile) of 3.5 inches at 500 yards at a 30-degree angle, and 4.25 inches at normal. At 2,000 yards, the shell pierces 2.44 and 3.03 inches. There is an AP 40 shot supplied for this gun, and a 12.5-pound HE shell.

(6) 75-mm AT Gun on a PzKw 2 Chassis

This 10-ton assembly may be recognized by the long-barreled gun with the muzzle brake, as in the previous description, but the PzKw 2 chassis has either five or six large bogie wheels. Its length is 15 ft. 2 in., width, 1 ft. 4 in., and height 16 ft. 6 in. With a 140-hp gasoline engine, the radius on the road is 118 miles, and cross country 78 miles. In front, the armor varies from .59 inch to 1.79

FIG. 4

inch, with .59 inch on the back and sides. The crew is probably four. The gun is the same one described in the previous paragraph.

(7) 76.2-mm (3-in) AT Gun on a 5-Ton Half-Track

Possibly another local improvisation, this piece of equipment consists of a Russian 76.2-mm gun mounted on the chassis of a 5-ton half-track in a high, square, box-like riveted structure of .20-inch armor, Open at the top (see figure 4). The gun may be employed both in field artillery and antitank roles.

The weight is about 10 tons. The mount is 19 ft. 9 in. long, 7 ft. 3 in. wide, and 10 ft. high. The motor is a 130-hp gasoline engine, giving the weapon a radius of action of 160 miles on roads and 70 across country, carrying a crew of probably six.

The 76.2-mm Russian field gun Model 36 (7.62-cm Pak 36 (r)) with a long, thin barrel throws a 14.8-pound capped armor-piercing shell at the relatively low velocity of 2,200 f/s, a 14-pound HE at 2,340 f/s, and an AP 40 shot of 9.25 pounds weight at 2,800 f/s. The range is not stated, but the firing charts include ranges up to 2,000 yards, at which range it is claimed that the AP shell will drive through 2.08 inches of armor with a 30-degree slope, and 2.52 inches, vertical. At 500 yards, the penetration is reported to be 3.11 and 3.70 inches, respectively. The awkward-appearing mount gives an unexpectedly large traverse of 60 degrees, with an elevation varying from minus 5 to plus 45 degrees. (The gun mount is capable of giving 75 degrees of elevation, but the shield fouls the front tarpaulin rail at 45 degrees.) Sixty-four rounds are carried, approximately half HE and half AP.

(8) 76.2-mm Gun on Tank Chassis

This is the 76.2-mm Russian gun just discussed, mounted on the light Czech PzKw 38(t) chassis with 4 bogies as described in Tactical And Technical Trends, No. 21, p. 6 (see figure 5); it is also mounted on the PzKw 2 chassis which has 5 bogie wheels. Both chassis are rather light for so large a gun. It seems unlikely that either the traverse or elevation on these tank chassis is as great as on the 5-ton half-track.

GERMAN SELF-PROPELLED 150-MM HOWITZER

Tactical and Technical Trends, No. 12, November 19, 1942.

The 150-mm medium howitzer, sFH 13, has been provided with a self-propelled mounting, the chassis of the French tracteur blindé 38L, made by Lorraine.

The sFH 13 is equipment of the last war, superseded in first-line units by the 15-cm sFH 18. Particulars of the gun are:
- Caliber: 149.7 mm
- Muzzle velocity: 1,250 f/s
- Maximum range: 9,300 yds
- Length of bore: 17 cals
- Number of grooves: 36
- Elevation: +5° to +45°
- Weight of projectile: 92.4 lbs

The particulars of the mount 38L are: length, 14 feet; width, 5 feet 2 inches; weight, 7 1/2 tons; engine, 70 horsepower; maximum speed, 22 miles per hour.

The sketch opposite shows the following details:

(a) A fixed gun-house of not very thick plate

(b) A limited traverse of not more than about 4 degrees

(c) A spade on the rear of the hull that can be let down to take recoil stresses.

It is notable that in this case an equipment firing a 92-lb shell to a maximum range of 9,300 yards has been mounted on a hull weighing no more than 7 1/2 tons.

This is another case in which the Germans have utilized a standard field gun to make self-propelled artillery. A recent picture shows another 150-mm howitzer, the 15-cm sIG 33, on a German Mark II chassis with the gun on a special mounting built into the hull. There is a three-sided shield no higher than the normal tank, instead of the very high box-like structure for the self-propelled sFH 13.

NEW AXIS SELF-PROPELLED GUNS

Tactical and Technical Trends, No. 18, Feb. 11, 1943.

Owing to the battlefield mobility of tanks, as well as to other factors, the towed antitank gun is not always an adequate antitank weapon. To supplement the towed gun, self-propelled antitank guns have been developed and organized into special units: for example, the U.S. tank-destroyer organizations. For a considerable period of time the Germans have shown a tendency to mount a large number of guns on self-propelled mounts, the calibers varying from 20 mm to 150 mm. Recently the following new German equipment of this type was reported to exist:

- German 37-mm AT gun on an armored personnel carrier;
- Russian 76.2 -mm gun on German Mark II tank chassis;
- Russian 76.2-mm gun on Czech light tank (38) chassis;
- German 75-mm tank gun (40) on German Mark II tank chassis;
- German 75-mm tank gun (40) on Czech light tank (38) chassis.

Of the above weapons, the first two are known to have been present in North Africa. Whether the last three have been issued to units is not known. The Germans are also reported to be developing 88-mm and 128-mm armored self-propelled guns.

The Italians are apparently still endeavoring to follow the Germans in the development of self-propelled weapons. It is reported that they now have a 90-mm self-propelled gun. While this gun is known to exist, it is not believed to have appeared yet in action. The Italian 75-mm self-propelled gun is reported to have proved not wholly successful, and it is thought that Italy does not possess sufficient resources to allow free improvisation on the German pattern.

NEW SELF-PROPELLED GUN
Intelligence Bulletin, October 1943

In Russia the Germans are using a new armored self-propelled gun, which bears at least an outward resemblance to the Pz. Kw. 6, the German tank often referred to as the "Tiger." The new self-propelled gun (see fig. 1) mounts an 88-mm cannon in a fixed turret, and has an over-all weight of 70 tons. Its maximum speed is reported to be not more than 12 miles per hour.

Although the armor of the new weapon, especially the front armor, is said to be harder to pierce than that of the Pz. Kw. 6, the Russians have found the former easier to set afire. They have nicknamed it the "Ferdinand."

A Russian staff officer makes the following observations regarding the performance of the "Ferdinand" on the Orel and Belgorod fronts, where the Germans, counterattacking, used a number of the new heavy weapons and Pz. Kw. 6's as battering rams in an attempt to force breaches in the Russian lines.

Figure 1a.—New German Heavy Self-propelled Gun (front view).

Figure 1b.—New German Heavy Self-propelled Gun (side and rear view).

During one battle the enemy assaulted our positions with 300 heavily armored vehicles, among them were about 50 "Tigers" and "Ferdinands." While the battle was taking place along our forward positions, 12 of our own heavy self-propelled guns remained hidden in their earth fortifications. When about, 20 "Tigers" and "Ferdinands" broke through our forward lines, our self-propelled artillery moved out from their concealed positions in order to fire by direct laying. An ambush was prepared near the threatened area, and the pieces were camouflaged.

Fire against the German armor was commenced when the attacking vehicles were about 500 yards away from our cannon.

Our first rounds were successful. At 500 yards "Tigers" suffered gaping holes in their turret armor and side armor. At 300 yards we pierced their frontal armor, and blew their turrets clean off. Hits on the side armor at this range nearly split the vehicles in half. It was somewhat different with the "Ferdinands." Their armor—the front armor, in particular—was more difficult to pierce, but their tracks, suspension, and side and turret, armor were no harder to damage and destroy than those of the "Tigers." The Germans lost at total of 12 "Tigers" and six "Ferdinands."

In another battle the same heavy armor of the enemy was engaged by our ordinary medium artillery, which used both special and regular ammunition. Three of our pieces were emplaced to form a triangle; they were reasonably far apart. This triangular disposition permitted unusually effective fire against "Ferdinands." Although the "Ferdinand's" fire is very accurate, its fixed turret does not permit it to shift its fire rapidly. When the gun is caught in a triangle, it is virtually helpless, because while it engages one cannon the other two take pot-shots at its vulnerable points. If the piece directly in front of a "Ferdinand" does not disclose its position by firing, the other two can usually dispose of the big gun with no loss to ourselves.

Obviously it is not always possible for us to arrange a battery in a triangle. Therefore, we require the closest possible cooperation between the pieces of a battery and also between neighboring batteries.

Point-blank fire from our medium tanks in ambush armed only with the 45-mm cannon, has taken care of many "Tigers" and "Ferdinands," as have land mines, Molotov cocktails, and cannon fire from our fighter planes.

It is also reported that the circular hole in the rear of the "Ferdinand's" fighting compartment is extremely vulnerable. This hole provides room for the recoil and the ejection of shells. Russian observers state that grenades or Molotov cocktails thrown into this opening can put the vehicle out of action.

Note: As the Intelligence Bulletin goes to press, further information regarding the "Ferdinand" has been made available.

It is reported that the crews consist of six men: A gun commander (usually a lieutenant, who is either a tank man or in artilleryman), a gunner, a driver-mechanic, a radio operator, and two additional gun crew members.

"Ferdinands" are organized in battalions called "Heavy Tank-Destroyer Battalions." Each battalion consists of three gun companies, a headquarters company, a repair company. and a transport column. Each gun company consists of three platoons of four guns each. The company headquarters has three guns, making a total of 14 guns per company. The battalion headquarters company has two guns, a Pz. Kw. 3, and four motorcycles.

On the offensive, the battalion moves in two echelons. The first echelon consists of two companies abreast, with each company in line and with a 100-yard interval between guns. The second echelon consists of the third company, also in line. The distance between echelons has not been reported.

Although the gun itself is excellent, the mounting has certain pronounced defects. (1) The gun can fire only to the front, and is effective only when stationary. (2) Poor vision from the fighting compartment allows more maneuverable tanks and antitank weapons to get in close to the gun.

NOTES ON GERMAN DIVISIONAL ARTILLERY

Tactical and Technical Trends,
No. 6, August 27, 1942.

The organization of the German divisional artillery, like that of our own, includes three battalions of 105-mm. howitzers, which ordinarily operate in direct support of the three infantry regiments, and one medium battalion. The medium battalion is composed of 2 batteries of 150-mm. howitzers and 1 battery of 100-mm. guns, and operates in general support of the division. There is also an infantry cannon company composed of six 75-mm. howitzers and two 150-mm. howitzers. In addition, in each armored and motorized division as well as certain assault infantry divisions, there is one armored assault artillery battalion composed of three 4-gun companies armed with self-propelled 75-mm. or 105-mm. howitzers.

In addition to this artillery there is in every division an artillery observation battalion which is composed of a sound-ranging battery and a flash-ranging battery (each separable into 2 independent platoons), a survey battery, a reproduction platoon, a signal platoon, and a meteorological section. This battalion works directly under the division artillery commander.

In general, the tactics and technique of German artillery are very similar to our own, but a recent report on cooperation between German artillery and other arms brings out several interesting divergences as well as some slight differences in emphasis.

All artillery orders are given orally at first; later those of the regiment and the division, particularly the latter, are confirmed and expanded in writing. The divisional artillery commander's order is not issued as an annex to the division order, but as a separate artillery order. Great stress is placed on the use of fragmentary and warning orders, and the Germans also emphasize that wherever possible orders should be given on terrain affording suitable observation rather than by reference to a map.

Counterbattery missions of the divisional medium artillery are heavily stressed. While counterbattery is primarily the task of the medium battalion, the other three battalions may often take over this function. The presence of the observation battalion is one of the reasons for emphasis on counterbattery as a divisional artillery function.

Great emphasis is also placed on the battalion as the fire-control unit, and the separation of the battalion into independent batteries to be used as attached artillery is never recommended except in extremely large sectors, or under very difficult terrain conditions such as thick woods.

In the preparation and conduct of fire, simplicity of technique is the goal. Generally a standard method is prescribed and followed, and variations are discouraged. This is typical of all German technique in that they deliberately adopt a simple method which will fit the large majority of cases, and consider that the gain in simplicity is more important than the loss of several highly refined techniques, each suitable for only a few complex situations. Reciprocal laying with the aiming circle is apparently the method most frequently used. It should be noted that this standardization of technique is in contrast to the general tactical doctrine of the Germans, which insists upon the uniqueness of each problem and the necessity for working out a complete and independent solution rather than applying a rigid prearranged formula.

Communications are normally by wire, and the use of radio is limited to periods of displacement. The one exception to this is the radio communication between observation posts and gun positions.

In preparation fires each battery normally covers one or more targets, each about 110 to 165 yards in width. At all times emphasis is placed on flexibility of fire plan and procedure, particularly by using irregular surprise fires on infantry and artillery, and on enemy command posts, as well as on the point of intended penetration.

The following table shows the maximum rates of fire consistent with efficient maintenance of materiel:

Weapons	Short bursts (rounds per minute)	Prolonged fire (rounds per minute)
100-mm. gun	5	1 1/2
105-mm. howitzer	6	2 1/2
150-mm. howitzer	4	1 1/3

Except in unusual circumstances the artillery "reserve" consists of a large supply of ammunition rather than uncommitted units.

In order to secure greater effect against personnel in the open, ricochet fire is deliberately sought by use of delayed fuse. With light howitzers ricochet is believed to be always obtainable up to an angle of impact of 270 mils, and usually obtainable up to 360 mils. The adjustment is secured with quick fuse, and fire for effect is conducted with delayed fuse. If for any reason the ricochet fire does not prove effective, fire for effect is continued with quick fuse.

The Germans believe in a "lone gun", placed at a sufficient distance from the rest of the battery so as to appear to be an entirely different position. This gun is used for harassing fire, fire against high targets, determination of weather corrections, and finally to deceive the hostile observation as to the true position of the battery.

It is essential that supported infantry commanders be generally familiar with the characteristics, capabilities, and limitations of artillery in order to secure most effective cooperation. They must understand: that the effectiveness of artillery depends to a great extent on the neutralization of enemy artillery, and that consequently some of the fire must be employed on counterbattery missions; that the ammunition supply is limited, and the laying of heavy concentrations on important areas means a loss of fire on less important ones; that the artillery should engage only those targets which justify its heavy fire; and finally that unnecessary or too hasty requests divert artillery from its principal missions and destroy mutual confidence.

One factor which insures that infantry commanders will be familiar with artillery capabilities and limitations is the presence of the infantry cannon company in the infantry regiment. This cannon company's presence also has several other effects. First of all, it settles the problem of the accompanying gun. Second, artillery is relieved of many small but difficult direct-support missions and is released for its larger missions. Third, and most important, it lessens the artillery-infantry gap which liaison officers are intended to bridge, since it means that the liaison is not between two distinct and separate units of artillery and infantry, but rather between the regular artillery of the supporting battalion and an infantry unit which already has organic artillery weapons. There is coordination of fire plans as well as mutual observation by the cannon company and the artillery. Also the divisional observation battalion lends its assistance the infantry cannon company.

It is essential that the infantry regimental and battalion commanders assist their cooperating artillery commander by continually informing him of the infantry plan of action, the infantry's progress, and its need for artillery support.

Infantry company, battalion, and regimental commanders are made "artillery minded" by being constantly trained to rely on artillery support to the utmost.

A very important function of the infantry is to seize and hold the forward locations necessary for artillery observation, thereby facilitating the artillery support. Likewise, the infantry should be informed of the positions of the artillery forward observers, observation posts, and command posts.

Finally, the closest support between the two arms is secured by having forward artillery observers operate with the advance infantry units. Forward observers with pack radio sets are believed to be the only effective means of obtaining satisfactory observation. Sets are used both by individual batteries and by battalions, and quite often the battery commander himself will act as forward observer, particularly at the beginning of an engagement when he is not familiar with the terrain. Alternate positions for all observation posts are stressed, and, as one of our observers reports "It is impossible to exaggerate the emphasis German doctrine puts on movement of observation posts and improvement of observation."

COMMENT: In summation the above article points out the following noteworthy features of German divisional artillery:

1. Early counterbattery fire by divisional artillery.
2. Use of battalion as a unit.
3. No set pattern for fire plan in preparations.
4. Ricochet fire.
5. Use of roving gun for registration, harassing fire, and deception.
6. Education of commanders of supported units as to value of—
    a. Neutralizing enemy artillery.
    b. Conservation of ammunition for important missions.
    c. Necessity for observation.
7. Close support through forward observers with advanced infantry, rather than through liaison detachments with supported unit commander.

OBSERVATIONS ON GERMAN ARTILLERY TACTICS

Tactical and Technical Trends, No. 31, August 12, 1943.

A recently returned American officer reports that in North Africa the Germans frequently made a practice of firing a few salvoes from a battery; then, moving out, about the time the American forward observers had the position taped. Our own guns would plaster the observed position only to find that the enemy guns, apparently on self-propelled mounts, opened fire from some other point.

An extremely clever trick was reported to have been turned by a German tank unit upon which a British 25-pounder (88 mm) battery was attempting to adjust. After the first salvo hit at some distance from the tanks, a second was fired which apparently fell wide, and the third salvo went wider; the forward observer was frantic.

This is what had happened: the German tanks had timed the first salvo from the report to the instant of burst, which can be done with a low-velocity piece such as the 25-pounder, and fired a salvo from their own guns so that their own shells burst on the ground some distance away from the tanks at the same moment when the battery's shells struck. The forward observer was attempting to correct his own fire from German shell bursts.

The most dangerous German artillery fire was not from HE bursting on impact, but HE time fuze air bursts, and ricochet fire. In this latter type of shelling, the projectiles would strike the ground and ricochet upward, bursting over the heads of the troops.

A rather surprising percentage of the German shells were duds. Whether this was caused by defective fuzes, or for the reason that the projectiles were AP, used when the supply of HE had been exhausted, was not known.

DECEPTIVE GERMAN ARTILLERY METHODS

Tactical and Technical Trends, No. 33, September 9, 1943.

In the following article translated from a recent issue of the "Red Star", some German methods of counteracting Russian sound and flash reconnaissance are examined. For a description of similar tactics see Tactical and Technical Trends, No. 31, p. 15.

* * *

Since the results of sound reconnaissance depend on atmospheric conditions, Germans always try to use these to their advantage. For example, when sound carries well, (at night, in fog, on calm days) Germans try to use their artillery as little as possible. On the other hand, when sound conditions favor the Germans (wind in the direction of their positions, vertical midday currents, sharp drops in temperature etc.) the activity of their artillery increases. In selecting their firing positions Germans take into consideration the effect of the surrounding terrain on sound. Firing positions on the reverse slopes of the hills, in groves, near lakes, and marshes are more desirable in this respect than those on tops of hills.

In order to deceive our sound reconnaissance and to draw our fire on empty positions Germans use "swinging" or "duty" batteries (American roving guns). These batteries swinging from one position to another, fire a few rounds from each position, mixing it occasionally with systematic fire. These positions are selected away from other batteries and other troop positions. Germans are very careful not to disclose their fire system. Many batteries do not fire for a long time as their mission is to ambush either our troops or our batteries. Almost never does a gun fire individually as it is then easily located by sound reconnaissance;

instead, as a rule, several batteries fire together at an even tempo so that individual shots are drowned in the general noise.

To camouflage fire activity of especially important positions special devices are used that imitate sounds of gunfire. These devices are placed from 200 to 300 meters on the flanks of the camouflaged battery, or to the rear with respect to the direction of actual firing. Sometimes, for more complete imitation of a battery, these devices are supplemented by others which produce a flash simultaneously with the real volley.

Along the same principle a single piece located also 200 to 300 meters from the others is used for ranging fire. This piece if moved farther away, would interfere with correct ranging for the rest of the battery and would also enable us to discover the trick. These seperate pieces also have the secondary mission of nuisance fire. If several batteries are to take part in a barrage, these ranging pieces are used during the first stages. As soon as the Germans think that our sound reconnaissance has located these pieces, the rest of the guns open up. The ranging pieces continue their fire until the end of the barrage.

In order to hide their guns from our flash locators, very often rockets are sent up, haystacks and other material burned, so that the gun flashes are nearly invisible against the burning background. Smokeless powder and flash hiders are also used. Large-scale engineering works are made in order to hide the batteries from ground and air observation. Each battery has two camouflage experts who supervise this work.

Of course, all these measures are not taken by every German battery all the time, but it is well to know about all these tricks. Such knowledge enables us to evaluate properly the findings of our flash and sound locators, and when everything else fails we check our evaluation with PW interrogation.

NOTES ON GERMAN ARTILLERY FORWARD OBSERVERS

Tactical and Technical Trends, No. 28, July 1, 1943.

In the observation of fire, the greatest reliance by the Germans is placed on forward observers. Often the battery commander himself goes ahead in this role. The part that the observer plays in German field operations is brought out in the following translation from a recent issue of Artilleristische Rundschau.

* * *

The artillery forward observer (Vorgeschobene Beobachter) plays a decisive part in the success of infantry. In the attack he goes along with the infantry, accompanied by a radio operator. If the attack is stopped, this observer calls for fire on enemy points of resistance and carries the infantry on to the next assault. In static warfare, the observer orders destructive fire against the enemy and covering fire to aid his own troops. He also directs destructive fire against enemy infantry who are about to attack or actually attacking. The results of this are shown not only in the effective cooperation between the two arms, but in the existence of a spirit of brotherhood in combat--the artillery forward observer becomes the best friend of the infantry.

A few examples from the Eastern Front will illustrate the role of the forward observer.

In one instance, a German battalion was attacking a Russian objective at a place where there was a churchyard in close proximity to the Russian rear; the attack was gaining ground very slowly, impeded by stubborn defense and by poor observation for the German artillery. Finally, a forward observer succeeded in the face of Russian fire in reaching an observation position located at the flank, whence he could observe the churchyard. The signal troops, working fast, established communication in a very short time with the battery, which was then able to deliver well-placed fire. The opponent was so pinned down that the attack regained its impetus. In a short time the village and churchyard were captured.

In August 1941, a German division had been defending for some time a stream south of C—. A battalion received the mission to make a limited-objective attack in order to secure prisoners; the attack was to be made with a reinforced company, supported by heavy infantry weapons and artillery. After assembly in combat outposts, the company began the attack in several groups. The forward observer of a light battery and heavy battery went forward with the company, while at the same time another forward observer was stationed in the advance combat positions of the sector to the right of the attack in order to watch for any threat to the flank. Given excellent support by the artillery, and working skillfully through the terrain, the assault troops succeeded in penetrating deeply into the Soviet positions, without loss, and in capturing prisoners and weapons. At the same time, on his own initiative, the company commander in the sector to the right sent a weaker assault group to capture a Russian scout squad. The forward artillery observer in this sector supported the effort so well that nearly all the personnel of the scout unit were disabled or captured. The result of these two operations was a total of 42 prisoners and 12 captured machine guns and mortars, while on the German side the only casualty was one soldier slightly wounded. The skillful and rapid fire-support given by the artillery as a result of the work of the forward observer played a major role in this success.

A forward observer showed up well in another local assault by a neighboring regiment. The night before the operation, he went into no-mans-land with a scout squad. Three kilometers in front of the German lines he found a hide-out, and for 9 hours observed the Russian position from so short a distance that no detail could be missed. He could look into each pit dug for protection against tanks and could almost count the number of occupants in each. The next morning the assault group attacked at the appointed time. The radio of the forward observer had scarcely given the first order of command when the answers roared from 3 batteries. The Russian position was thoroughly raked. After a momentary pause, a powerful concentration of fire was placed on the left-hand sector of the enemy positions, only to move in another instant 100 yards to the right on a zigzag trench net. On the left, where the dust clouds from the bursts were slowly settling, the hand grenades of the assault troops were already exploding. With incredible speed, the trenches were mopped up, and always, throughout the action, the concentrated fire of 12 guns moved just before the assault group from right to left. About 500 meters of the Russian position was overrun in this way. With the mission accomplished, the assault group withdrew from the Russian positions, while the forward artillery observer placed his fire to cover the withdrawal. Numerous prisoners and weapons were brought in, without any losses suffered by the Germans. In this case too, the service of the forward artillery observer was no minor factor.

Every member of the First Battalion still remembers the day at O-- in September 1941. This position was taken by storm without any difficulty. However, before the battalion had organized itself for defense, the Russians made a counter-attack in heavy force, supported by 18 tanks and designed to recover the locality. Fortunately, the second battery which had been attached to the battalion had moved its position and was ready for action, having established communications with the forward observer. Gun after gun fired its destructive barrage into the massed ranks of the Russian infantry following the tanks. Even the tanks hesitated, and then gave up the attack. The Russian attack was repeated several times in very strong force, and every time was stopped by the barrage ordered and directed by the forward observer. Bodies of Russians and ruined tanks covered the field at evening, and the battalion officers thanked the battery commander, assuring him that the village would have fallen had it not been for the artillery support and the courageous conduct of the forward observer, who had fallen in the combat.

GERMAN ANTIAIRCRAFT ARTILLERY

Military Intelligence Service,
Special Series 10, Feb. 1943

SECTION I. ORGANIZATION

1. General

The German approach to the subject of military organization is one of extreme flexibility. The underlying thought is that in view of the rapid progress of science as applied to war, organizational practice must remain flexible if it is to take advantage promptly of new scientific development, to exploit various kinds of situations, and to cope with all types of enemies. Efficient combat effectiveness of an organization is always considered a primary requisite. It should therefore be remembered that although the organization of German antiaircraft units is founded on certain basic principles, experimentation with new tactical doctrines, economy of military manpower and equipment, or the considered needs of a task force situation may cause the organization of certain AA units to vary from normal.

2. Basic Principles of Organization

All German military organization is based on certain fundamental principles which are primarily designed to permit tactical and administrative flexibility.

One of these fundamentals is the *Einheit* (unit) principle, which provides that any given arm or service will develop a number of standard unit groups, each with standard organization, leadership, training, and equipment. The unit group is an organic entity, capable of operating independently and self-sufficient both for tactical and administrative purposes. Within a given branch or service, each basic type of unit group will represent a different combination of the various components (or weapons) of that branch or service. In AA organization the unit groups are ordinarily battalions, and the types (heavy, mixed, light, etc.) differ in organic composition with respect to their respective weapons (light and/or heavy guns, searchlights, etc.).

The *Einheit* principle of organization has several advantages. Obviously the supply and replacement of equipment can be more readily geared to a few standard types of units. The training and tactical employment of a given type of unit can be standardized, and directed with uniformity. Above all, the existence of these basic type-units, each so composed as to serve a different function, permits easy organization of any desired type of larger unit. In the AA branch, for example, regiments are formed by combining any desired number of the different basic units. And the *Einheit* system is excellently designed to facilitate the construction of task forces, made up of different amounts of necessary arms and services, in terms of the basic units of each arm or service required for a given mission.

3. Antiaircraft as a Component of the Air Force
a. General

With some few exceptions, German antiaircraft units are an organic part of the German Air Force (*Luftwaffe*). German antiaircraft artillery is called *Flakartillerie*, and is more commonly referred to as "Flak." This term is an abbreviation of "*Fl*ieger- or *Fl*ug*a*bwehr*k*anone," which means "cannon for defense against aviation."

Flak troops wear the uniform of the Luftwaffe, which is easily distinguished from that of the Army and Navy by the gray-blue color of the material, the lounge cut of the open collar blouse, and the plain trousers. To distinguish the AA artillery from other branches of the Air Force, red piping is worn on the cap, and the blouses of both officers and enlisted men have this distinguishing red color on the shoulder strap as lining and edging, and on the collar patches.

Flak serving in the field is fully motorized, and units intended to operate with the spearhead of the attack are equipped for cross-country operation.

Luftwaffe AA organizations and units operating with the Army are subordinated operationally and for command purposes to the Army unit concerned, and administratively (for replacements, etc.) to a parent Air Force ground unit.

b. Higher Units

(1) *General.*—In general, Flak units consist of corps, divisions, regiments, battalions, and batteries. From a practical point of view the AA corps, divisional, and regimental organizations are primarily composed of a commander, staff, and organizational troops who coordinate and assist in the disposition and activities of the basic units, the battalions (*Abteilungen*).

(2) *Corps.*—The *Flakkorps* is the highest AA unit. It may be found in rear areas or with field forces, depending on the considered need for a command of this size. There is no fixed allotment of units to this highest formation; it has been noted that the corps may contain from two to four AA divisions. In general, when serving with the field forces, an AA corps would normally control the area of an army group (group of armies). It may also be found with air fleets and on some occasions with Panzer armies.

(3) *Division.*—The *Flakdivision* is frequently found in German armies. Its composition is not fixed, varying from two to five regiments. In general, when with field forces, the AA division usually operates in the area of an army.

(4) *Regiment.*—(a) *Pre-war establishment.*—At the outbreak of World War II, Flak regiments were organized on a standard basis of three battalions per regiment. The first two battalions were alike, each consisting of three batteries of heavy AA guns and two batteries of light AA guns with organic 60-cm (light) searchlights. The third battalion consisted of three batteries, each with nine 150-cm (heavy) searchlights.

(b) *Present organization.*—At the present time the composition of the regiment is flexible; it may contain from three to five battalions of any type.

c. The Battalion

(1) *General.*—The basic tactical AA unit is the battalion (*Abteilung*), which also has administrative functions. There are several known types of gun battalions, but in general these types will fall into one of three general categories consisting of heavy, mixed, and light battalions. In this connection, it should be noted that in action the gun battalion commander is essentially a tactical commander, the battery being the fire-control unit. Allotment of AA units to Army field forces varies according to the estimated needs, but all army corps commonly has one or more separate gun battalions permanently attached to it during all operations, and at least one mixed battalion will usually be found attached to a Panzer division.

(2) *Heavy battalion.*—This battalion is equipped with either 88-mm or 105-mm antiaircraft guns, or with both, and usually consists of a headquarters with three batteries (*Batterien*) each of four, or possibly six, guns. This type of organization is rare; the unit is usually found only in static positions in Germany.

(3) *Mixed battalion.*—This is the more common type of standard battalion organization incorporating heavy AA guns. There are two separate establishments for these mixed battalions, one with four 88-mm guns per battery, the other with six. The most recent indications suggest that preference is being shown for the six-gun unit as equipment becomes available. In some cases, primarily in rear areas, 105-mm AA guns may be substituted for the 88-mm guns.

The organization of this mixed battalion is as follows:
- Headquarters;
- 3 heavy batteries, each consisting of four (possibly six) 88-mm guns, and two 20-mm guns for close protection;
- 2 light batteries, each consisting of twelve 20-mm guns and

four 60-cm (23.58-inch) searchlights. (A medium battery of nine 37-mm guns and four 60-cm searchlights is sometimes substituted for one of the light batteries.)

(4) *Light battalion.*—Two types of light gun battalions exist:
  (a) Headquarters;
    3 light batteries, each of twelve 20-mm guns;
    1 searchlight battery of sixteen 60-cm searchlights.
  (b) Headquarters;
    2 light batteries, each of twelve 20-mm guns;
    1 medium battery of nine 37-mm guns;
    1 searchlight battery of sixteen 60-cm searchlights.

(5) *Reserve battalion.*—In addition to the battalions mentioned above, there are heavy, mixed, and light reserve battalions. These have only a small amount of organic motor transport and are used in a static role in Germany and rear areas. Otherwise the reserve organization corresponds to that of standard mobile battalions. The transportation of these battalions, when necessary, is carried out by a separate transport unit.

(6) *Searchlight battalion.*—Most searchlight battalions are composed of a headquarters and three batteries, each battery containing nine 150-cm (60-inch) searchlights. Sound locators are used with these searchlights, and although their present number per battery varies with the employment of the searchlights in rear areas, at the beginning of the war they were allotted on the basis of one per searchlight. Although mobile, most of the heavy searchlight battalions are used only within rear and static defense areas. The smaller, 60-cm (23.58-inch) lights are used with 20-mm and 37-mm AA guns, and accordingly are an organic part of both the light and mixed battalion, as mentioned above. Heavy searchlight battalions are very often grouped to form searchlight regiments, which operate as such only in rear areas.

d. The Battery

(1) *General.*—The battery (*Batterie*) is the normal fire unit of AA

artillery. Several types of batteries exist:

(2) *Heavy battery.*—A heavy battery in the mixed battalion is normally organized as follows:
  (a) Combat echelon, consisting of—
    Battery headquarters,
    Gun and instrument detachments,
    Communication detachments,
    Light Flak section,
    Ammunition detachment,
    Combat train.
  (b) Ration transport.
  (c) Baggage transport.

(3) *Light and medium battery.*—A light battery in a mixed battalion comprises four gun sections and one 60-cm searchlight section of four searchlights (one searchlight is normally allotted to each gun section), and is subdivided as follows:
  (a) Combat echelon, consisting of—
    Battery headquarters,
    Gun and searchlight detachments,
    Communication detachment,
    Ammunition detachment,
    Combat train.
  (b) Ration transport.
  (c) Baggage transport.

(4) *Searchlight battery.*—The heavy searchlight battery is usually organized as follows:
  (a) Combat echelon, consisting of—
    Battery headquarters,
    Searchlight detachments,
    Communication detachment,
    Combat train.
  (b) Ration transport.
  (c) Baggage transport.

The exact employment of the light 60-cm searchlight batteries is not known, but it is believed that the battery is subdivided into sections to permit employment of individual detachments with gun sections. This practice is somewhat similar to the system used with searchlights which are an organic part of the light gun batteries of mixed battalions. In the latter case, the four searchlights in the section are broken down into four detachments, thus allowing one light searchlight for each gun section.

e. The Zug

The closest U.S. military equivalent of the *Zug* is "platoon." It is the smallest operational unit above the single gun and ordinarily applies only to the light or medium gun platoon of three guns, although in rare cases two heavy guns may operate as a platoon. In the heavy searchlight battery, there are usually three platoons of three lights each.

f. Railway Flak Units

Antiaircraft guns are also mounted on railway cars. Railway Flak units are organized into regiments, battalions, and batteries. The precise composition of the units is not known, but it is believed that the regimental organization forms a pool from which units may be drawn as necessity arises, either for mobile defense or for train-protection purposes. Although Railway Flak units are part of the Air Force and are administered through the usual Air Force channels, it is probable that train-protection detachments are operationally subordinate to the transport authorities. There is also some evidence that AA guns provided for the defense of military trains may in certain circumstances be manned by organic Army personnel. It is interesting to note that the AA guns on railway mounts may be light or heavy, and may consist of any of the following calibers: 20-mm (single- or four-barreled), 37-mm, 75-mm (probably), 88-mm, 105-mm, and possibly even the 150-mm.

4. Antiaircraft Organic to the Army

a. General

Although German AA artillery as an arm is an organic part of the

Air Force, there are independent AA battalions which belong to the infantry and artillery of the Army, and are therefore organically a part of the German Army ground forces. The general term *Heeresflak* is applied to these independent units when distinguishing them, in staff tables or on orders of battle in chart form, as a category distinct from other troops, and also when referring to organic Army AA troops as distinguished from the standard Air Force AA troops. Actually, the term *Heeresflak* covers two distinct types of units: the *Flabataillon*[1] and the *Heeresflak Abteilung*. The term *Fla* is an abbreviation of "*Fl*ug*a*bwehr," which means "AA defense."

b. Fla Battalion

Flabataillon troops belong to the infantry arm and wear its distinctive white piping. There are two different types of Fla battalions: the battalion of six companies in which the company apparently is the tactical unit, and the battalion of three companies in which the battalion itself is the tactical unit, although its companies may on occasion be found operating independently. The Fla battalion is equipped with standard machine guns, and either 20-mm (both single- and four-barreled) or 37-mm AA guns, all on self-propelled mounts. These guns are available for additional use in antitank or other roles against ground targets.

c. Heeresflak Abteilung

Heeresflak Abteilung troops belong to the artillery arm and wear its distinctive red piping. *Heeresflak* battalions are mechanized, and in most cases consist of three heavy batteries each of four 88-mm guns, and two light batteries each of either twelve 20-mm guns or nine 37-mm guns. All equipment may be used in AA and in antitank or other ground roles.

d. Operational Control

The operational control of these special types of AA units is extremely flexible. Although they are normally allotted from a GHQ pool to an army, army corps, or division for permanent

---

[1] The Fla "battalion" is ordinarily referred to in German military usage as Bataillon rather than by the more customary term Abteilung (see below).

organic AA protection, they have been known to be subordinated to Luftwaffe Flak divisions and regiments.

5. Antiaircraft in the Navy

The German Navy mans AA artillery in certain coastal forts. Except for being emplaced on permanent mounts, these AA guns do not differ materially from the normal Flak armament, and the same applies to AA guns on board ships. From the point of view of organization of rear-area defenses, it should be noted that the AA armament in these coastal forts, as well as the AA guns on board Navy ships undergoing repair or at rest in harbor, is used at need as a part of the AA ground defense of the immediate area.

SECTION II. WEAPONS AND EQUIPMENT

6. Trend of Development

a. Historical

With the tremendous strides in development of combat aviation during the period between World War I and World War II, it became increasingly evident that a corresponding development of AA materiel and tactics was quite necessary. Although the Germans were limited in their military establishment as a result of World War I, they nevertheless conducted extensive research and tests to develop new AA materiel. During this post-war period, also, came experiments with mechanized armored vehicles, and new doctrine as to the possibilities of their employment. Under the circumstances, it was only logical that some experimentation should take place with the object of designing a gun which could be used against either aircraft or mechanized ground vehicles. In 1936 the Spanish Civil War gave the Germans a chance to test their first efforts along these lines; in 1939 the campaign in Poland permitted a full test of the refined product, and results were used as a guide on which to base standardization and further development. The later campaign in France and other campaigns have, of course, served as further proving grounds.

b. Mobility

One of the main results of the battle experiences of the Germans has been vindication of the concept that AA guns used in any but purely static positions must be highly mobile, and that even in static situations it is to the best interests of protection against hostile aircraft to have a certain proportion of the AA artillery defenses in a highly mobile state for purposes of flexibility. Furthermore, the increased use of AA weapons with mobile units in the field has given a great spur to development of AA mobility.

c. Dual-Purpose Construction

With the practical tests of 1936 in the Spanish Civil War came the realization that with some modifications the then current AA weapons would have definite possibilities as effective antitank weapons. This finding was the more acceptable in view of the German military precept of acting on the offense wherever possible. The possibility of employing AA guns in forward areas in an offensive role definitely removed them from the status of defensive weapons and placed them in the category of important offensive weapons. The Polish Campaign, the French Campaign, and the early successes of Rommel in the Libyan Desert are eloquent proofs of the increasing development and use of AA weapons against mechanized ground targets. It should be remembered, of course, that AA gunnery demands weapons with a high rate of fire, rapid fire-control calculation, fast tracking speeds, and a high muzzle velocity. These factors contributed materially in the decision to adapt these weapons to an AT role. The original difficulty in making these AA weapons dual-purpose rested mainly in securing a satisfactory mobile carriage or mount which could withstand equally well the shock and recoil of high-elevation AA fire, and of horizontal and subhorizontal fire.

d. Multipurpose Use

With satisfactory development and use of the AA gun as an AT weapon came the logical discovery that the main AA/AT weapons could be used against targets other than aircraft or tanks. Thus we hear of the 88-mm guns being used against fortified gun positions, as well as for the direct support of ground troops, for interdiction fire against enemy communications, and for fire against river and coastal targets. We even hear of its being mounted on U-boats. As a result of these and similar experiences, German field commanders have found AA artillery to be one of their most useful weapons, and there is evidence of a trend suggesting that German artillery of the future, up to a certain caliber, will include an even greater proportion of AA weapons placed on multipurpose mounts.

e. German Classification of Flak Weapons

Although Flak weapons are generally referred to by the United Nations as light Flak and heavy Flak, probably because of the classification of AA *Abteilungen* into heavy (mixed) and light units, the Germans divide their Flak guns into the three general classifications: light, medium, and heavy. Light guns include only the various types of 20-mm Flak weapons; medium guns include the 37-mm, 40-mm, 47-mm, and reported 50-mm Flak weapons; and heavy Flak consists of the 75-mm, 88-mm, 105-mm, 127-mm, and 150-mm weapons. Of these guns, only the 20-mm, 37-mm, 88-mm, 105-mm, and 150-mm are used by the Germans to any great extent.

7. Types of AA Guns

a. 7.92-mm Standard Machine Gun

(1) *Description.*—The Germans now use one standard machine gun to fill all roles; namely, the air-cooled 7.92-mm (.31-inch) MG 34. This is considered a light machine gun when used with its light bipod, and a heavy machine gun when used with the heavy tripod mount. It is fitted in special single and dual mounts for AA purposes, and is also found in armored cars, carriers, and tanks. It fires all the types of 7.92-mm (.31-inch) ammunition which the German rifles and aircraft machine guns use. But lately there has been a marked emphasis on the use of armor-piercing ammunition in all 7.92-mm weapons. Belt

Figure 3.—2-cm (20-mm) AA/AT gun 30 in action.

feed is normally employed for the machine gun, but it is quite common for two or more 50-round belts to be joined end to end, thus reducing the delays involved in the changing of belts. A special belt drum, holding one 50-round belt compactly coiled within it, may be fitted on the left of the gun when the weapon is used as a light machine gun or for AA purposes. The gun weighs 15 1/2 pounds without the mount. The barrel is changed after each 250 rounds of continuous fire.

(2) *Use in AA Role.*—On the AA amount, this machine gun is used organically by all branches of the German Army for local protection against low-flying aircraft. It supplements the fire furnished by rifles. Strictly speaking, this weapon is not classed as a Flak weapon, the 20-mm cannon usually being considered the smallest caliber in the Flak class.

b. 20-mm AA/AT Gun (Models 30 and 38) (figs. 3 and 4)

(1) *Description.*—The 2-cm[2] Flak 30 (.79-inch) was introduced into the German Navy in 1930 and into the German Air Force

---

2 The German practice is to designate gun types in terms of centimeters rather than millimeters, and in all references made hereafter, the German style will be followed in the paragraphs concerned with descriptions of particular weapons.

Figure 4.—2-cm (20-mm) AA/AT gun 38 in action on self-propelled mount.

in 1935. It has been the main armament of light AA units, and can be used in an antitank role. The gun is fed by a flat box-magazine containing 20 rounds, and is recoil-operated. It has a detachable barrel, and is provided with automatic and single-shot mechanisms. The trigger mechanism is pedal-operated. The gun may be mounted on road or railway vehicles.

It is normally transported on a single-axle trailer. This trailer may be drawn by motor transport or by horse, and is easily manhandled. The gun and its mount may also be split into loads for transport in particularly difficult country. The gun is normally fired with its mount on the ground and with the trailer removed. It can, however, be fired from the trailer in an emergency (i.e., on the march), rough traverse being obtained by pushing the trailer around.

A later version of the model 30 is contained in the 2-cm Flak 38, which does not differ materially from the earlier version apart from having higher theoretical and practical rates of fire. Particulars pertaining to the 2-cm Flak 38 are as follows:

- Muzzle velocity (HE): 2,950 f/s
- Muzzle velocity (AP): 2,720 f/s
- Maximum horizontal range: 5,230 yds
- Maximum vertical range: 12,465 ft
- Maximum effective ceiling with self-destroying tracer ammunition.: 7,215 ft with 6 secs time of flight
- Theoretical rate of fire (rpm): (Model 30: 280), Model 38: 420–480
- Practical rate of fire (rpm): (Model 30: 120), Model 38 (estimated): 180–220
- Weight in action: 906 lbs
- Weight in draft: 1,650 lbs
- Elevation: -12° to +90°
- Traverse: 360°
- Length of barrel: 65 cals (51.2 inches)
- Ammunition—three classes, as follows:

    (i) Self-destroying HE tracer with percussion fuze (weight of projectile, 4.1 ounces; weight of complete round, 10.6 ounces)

    (ii) AP tracer (weight of projectile, 5.2 ounces; weight of complete round, 11.6 ounces)

    (iii) Practice (HE and AP)

    Normally the penetration performance with AP is 45 mm (1.77 inches) of armor at 100 yards.

(2) *Sights.*—The two alternative sights normally used with the 2-cm Flak 30 are the *Flakvisier* 35 and the *Linealvisier* 21, both of which are also used with the 2-cm Flak 38. A newer sight, known as the *Flakvisier* 38, has been developed for use with the 2-cm Flak 38.

It should be noted that all these sights are dependent on some separate continuous and accurate means of providing range. For this purpose, each gun detachment includes a range-taker who is equipped with a portable 1-meter-base stereoscopic range-finder.

In addition, a simple telescopic sight may be used with either the 2-cm Flak 30 or the 2-cm Flak 38.

- (a) *Flakvisier (AA Sight) 35.*—This is a reflecting-mirror sight with a computor mechanism operating on the course-and-speed principle. If the target is kept in the center of the sight, and the appropriate settings for slant range, speed, and course and angle of dive or climb are set in, then the bore of the gun is in correct alignment to pass the shell through the future position of the target. The setting for course is by means of a pointer in the horizontal plane which is kept parallel to the estimated course of the aircraft. The setting for angle of dive or climb is by means of a pointer set in the vertical plane.
- (b) *Flakvisier (AA Sight) 38.*—Information about the *Flakvisier* 38 is at present very incomplete, but what is known shows that it represents a departure from the course-and-speed principle on which the *Flakvisier* 35 functions. This sight can be used both against air targets, and against moving and fixed land and sea targets.

The *Flakvisier* 38 is an electric automatic sight. The layer keeps a cross on his object glass coincident with the target, thus obtaining angle of sight and azimuth. Range, either estimated or called out by the range-taker, is set by the range-setter.

The sighting arrangement consists of illuminated cross wires automatically controlled in terms of super-elevation and deflections. The elevating and traversing gears are coupled to elevating and traversing tachometer-dynamos in such a way that the voltages generated by them vary with the speeds of laying.

The gun's traversing gear is coupled to a tachometer-dynamo, which produces electric voltage varying directly with the rate of traverse. The terminals are connected to a moving coil meter which measures the strength of the electric current. A variable resistance depending on range setting is introduced, so that the current is regulated both by the tachometer-dynamo and by the strength of the range resistance. With short ranges the corresponding resistance is low and the deflection large; with long ranges, the deflection is small and the resistance high. The resultant lateral deflection is transmitted to the layer's vertical cross wire, which moves in the direction opposite to the course of the aircraft.

Vertical deflection is obtained by multiplying the rate of change of the angle of sight by the time of flight of the shell. Rate of change is measured by the rate of elevation or depression of the gun, whereas time of flight is taken as a measure of the range set. Superelevation in terms of range is added to the vertical deflection to give the appropriate quadrant elevation. The resultant value is automatically applied to the layer's horizontal cross wire.

- (c) *Linealviser (Linear Sight) 21 (figs. 6).* — This is a form of direct AA sight, giving course, speed, and range adjustment. It consists of a horizontal bar which is graduated from 0 to 1,600 meters. Range is set by turning a cylindrical hand nut on the runner of a cartwheel-type foresight, thus increasing the "lead" as the range is increased.

The ring foresight is rotatable, thus enabling course of the target to be set. A bar showing speed from 11 to 150 meters per second is mounted moveably on the foresight. This speed bar can also be adjusted to the angle of dive or climb. The backsight consists of an aperture set between two layers of nonsplintering glass inclined at 45 degrees to the horizontal bar.

Both the *Flakvisier* 35 and the *Flakvisier* 38 must be removed before the *Linealvisier* 21 can be mounted.

- (d) *Telescopic sight.* — A simple telescopic sight (with a magnification of eight) may also be employed for the engagement of armored vehicles and ground targets.

(3) *1-meter-base range-finder (fig. 7).* — The 1-meter (39.37-inch)-base range-finder is employed by light AA detachments manning the 2-cm Flak 30 and 38 and the 3.7-cm Flak 36.

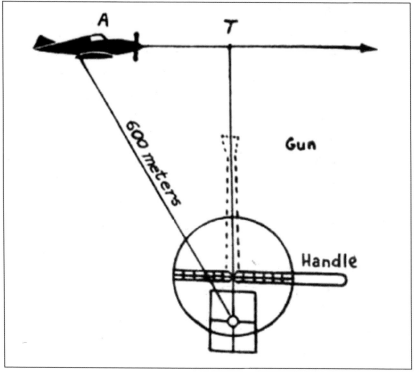

Figure 6.—Sighting the target with Linealvisier 21.

Magnification is sixfold, and the range is from 800 to 26,200 feet. This instrument is normally used strapped to the rangetaker's shoulders, but there is also provision for a small tripod.

    1. Bracket.
    2. Suspension claws.
    3. Clamping screw.
    4. Slit guide.
    5. Backsight bracket.
    6. Backsight.
    7. Slide.
    8. Ring foresight.
    9. Range knob.
    10. Driving disk.
    11. Backsight retaining springs.
    12. Rule.
    13. Aiming line.

14. Setting handle.

15. Speed scale.

The instrument is manufactured by Carl Zeiss of Jena. It is of the standard stereoscopic pattern, estimation of distance being by means of two reticles, one in each eyepiece, which when "fused" stereoscopically appear superimposed upon the image in depth. The instrument is difficult to handle, and considerable practice is necessary before an operator can obtain satisfactory results. The operator is required to produce accurate results at slant ranges up to 4,000 meters (4,400 yards)

(4) *Personnel*. The gun detachment consists of seven men as follows:
- Detachment Commander
- No. 1 : Layer
- No. 2 : Range-setter
- No. 3 : Course-setter
- No. 4 : Loader
- No. 5 : Range-taker
- Vehicle driver

c. 20-mm Four-Barreled AA/AT Gun (Quadruple Mount) (Fig. 8)

(1) *Description.*—The 2-cm *Flakvierling* 38 consists of four 2-cm Flak 38 guns. It may be employed either against aerial or ground targets. It is normally transported on a special trailer, but may also be mounted on half-track vehicles or railway mounts.

There is also a static version for use on Flak towers, in coast defenses, etc. In the trailer version, the gun is normally fired with its mount on the ground and with the trailer removed. It can, however, be fired front the trailer in an emergency (i.e., on the march). A traverse of only about 10 degrees at top elevation is possible in this position. Two foot-levers operate the trigger mechanism. Each foot-lever actuates the triggers of two diametrically opposite guns (i.e., the top left and the bottom right, and the top right and bottom left). This arrangement

Figure 7.—1-meter-base range-finder in use with 3.7-cm (37-mm) AA/AT gun.

provides uninterrupted, continuous fire. While two guns are firing, the magazines of the other two can be changed. When both firing levers are operated, all four guns fire simultaneously. Furthermore, should there be a stoppage on one or more guns, the remaining guns can continue to fire. Provision is made for single-shot or continuous fire on each weapon. A shield may be fitted to the carriage. This weapon fires the same ammunition as does the 2-cm Flak 38 described above.

The following additional characteristics pertain to the four-barreled mount:
- Theoretical rate of fire: 1,680-1,920 rpm
- Practical rate of fire (estimated): 700-800 rpm
- Elevation: -10° to +100°
- Traverse: 360°
- Rate of traverse (two speed): 7 1/2° or 22 1/2° (per turn of handwheel)
- Rate of elevation (two speed): 4° or 12° (per turn of handwheel)
- Loading: By flat box-magazines containing 20 rounds in two staggered rows
- Weight in action (mobile version): 2,979 lbs
- Weight in draft (with accessories): 4,866 lbs
- Weight of trailer 52: 1,848 lbs
- Weight in action (static version): 1.25 tons

(2) *Sights.*—The equipment is provided with the *Flatvisier* 40 (or, where not available, *Linealvisier* 21—see b (2) (c), above), and a telescopic sight for the engagement of ground targets (see b (2) (d), above). The *Flakvisier* 40 operates on the same principle as the *Flakvisier* 38, described in b (2) (b), above. Apparently, *Flakvisier* 35 may also be used on the 2-cm *Flakvierling* 38.

d. 37-mm AA/AT Gun (figs. 7 and 9)

(1) *Description.*—The 3.7-cm (1.45-inch) Flak 36 is the smallest caliber of medium Flak artillery. This gun is mounted on a two-wheeled trailer, detached when the gun is in the firing position, but the gun can be fired from the trailer in an emergency. This method can be adopted both in an AT and an AA role on the march; movement in azimuth is, however, very limited under these conditions, and the crew may have to move the gun and trailer bodily to enable the target to be engaged.

When on the trailer, the gun is towed behind motor transportation in which the personnel and stores are also carried. This gun also is found on self-propelled half-track

Figure 8.—2-cm (20-mm) Flakvierling 38 on fixed support, showing ammunition feed.

vehicles and on railway mounts. Other characteristics of this gun are as follows:
- Muzzle velocity: 2,690 f/s
- Maximum horizontal range: 8,744 yds

Figure 9.—Demonstration class inspecting 3.7-cm (37-mm) AA/AT gun. (The German instructor is pointing to the feed mechanism.)

- Maximum vertical range: 15,600 ft
- Theoretical rate of fire: 150 rpm
- Practical rate of fire: 60 rpm
- Maximum effective ceiling with self-destroying tracer

ammuniion. (A new shell has been introduced, which is self-destroying at 9,185-11,480 ft. after 7-10 secs.): 13,775 ft with 14 secs time of flight
- Automatic, recoil-operated; the firing mechanism can be set for single-shot or continuous fire as required. The ammunition is loaded in clips holding 6 rounds.
- Weight in action: 3,100 lbs (approx.)
- Elevation: -10° to +85°
- Traverse: 360°
- Length of barrel: 50 cals (6 ft)
- Ammunition—two classes, as follows:
  (i) Self-destroying HE tracer vvith percussion fuze (weight of projectile, 1 lb. 6 oz)
  (ii) AP tracer (weight of projectile, 1 lb 8 1/2 oz)

(2) *Sights.*—The *Flakvisier* 33 is normally used for AA fire with this Weapon. This sight is believed to be similar in principle to the *Flakvisier* 35 used with the 2-cm Flak 30, described above. Observation by tracer is used with this sight for close targets where the angular velocity is high; in such cases, only the course is set into the sight.

(3) *Personnel.*—The gun detachment consists of 12 men as follows:
- Detachment Commander
- No. 1 : Layer
- N0. 2 : Range-setter
- No. 3 : Course-setter
- No. 4 : Loader
- No. 5 : Range-taker
- No. 6 : | Ammunition numbers
- No. 7 : |
- Vehicle driver
- Vehicle driver's relief
- Spotters (2)

e. 40-mm AA Gun

Although used by the Germans, the 4-cm (1.57-inch) Flak 36 iS not encountered very often in German AA units. The few guns known to be in the hands of the Germans are believed to have been taken for the most part from the Polish Army after the Polish Campaign. The 4-cm Flak 36 is a Bofors gun, having characteristics similar to the weapon used by the British except for some few variations in performance characteristics. A few characteristics of this gun are as follows:

- Muzzle velocity: 2,950 f/s
- Maximum horizontal range: 12,300 yds
- Maximum vertical range: 23,200 ft
- Effective ceiling: 16,200 ft
- Theoretical rate of fire: 120 rpm
- Practical rate of fire: 80 rpm
- Weight of projectile: 2.2 lbs
- Weight in action: 4,234 lbs
- Elevation: -5° to +90°
- Traverse: 360°
- Length of barrel: 60 cals

f. 47-mm AA Gun

The 4.7-cm Flak 37 has in the past been used to some extent by the Germans as a medium AA/AT gun, but there are indications that the Germans are not entirely satisfied with its performance, and that no attempt will be made to produce this gun any large quantity, This weapon is a Czech model, having originally been produced at the Skoda works and adopted for use by the Czechoslovakian Army, The gun is tractor-drawn, but it is also found on some self-propelled mounts. A few of the characteristics are as follows:

- Muzzle velocity: 2,620 f/s
- Maximum horizontal range: 10,350 yds
- Maximum vertical range: 22,300 ft
- Maximum effective ceiling: 17,000 ft
- Theoretical rate of fire: 25 rpm

- Practical rate of fire: 15 rpm
- Weight in action: 3,400 lbs (approx.)
- Elevation: -10° to +85°
- Traverse: 360°
- Weight of projectile: 3.3 lbs

g. 50-mm AA AT Gun

The 5-cm Flak 41 (1.97-inch) has only recently been brought into service. Its introduction indicates a considered need for a medium gun with a higher ceiling and greater destructive power than the standard medium 3.7-cm. No detailed or accurate information is available about its performance, but it is claimed by the Germans to fire both HE and AP ammunition and to be provided with a new Flak sight 41, which, according to a sketchy German report, is operated by one man and is a completely automatic clockwork-sight. Also according to the report, range is introduced and angular velocities are calculated in such a way that superelevation and vertical and lateral deflections are automatically applied.

This reported new gun should not be confused with the 5-cm Pak[3] 41, which is purely an AT weapon,

h. 75-mm AA Gun

The 7.5-cm Flak L/60 is a 1938 model, and is only slightly modified from the 7.5-cm Flak L/59, which is a 1934 model. The 7.5-cm Flak L/60 is carried on a trailer mount and is ordinarily tractor-drawn, Some versions of this gun may also be found on self-propelled mounts, and in fixed AA installations. The weapon is not used to any great extent, however, since the 88-mm gun has become the standard German gun of this class, just as the U.S. 90-mm AA gun is superseding the U.S. 3-inch AA gun. Some of the characteristics of the 7.5-cm Flak L/60 are as follows:

- Muzzle velocity: 2,780 f/s
- Maximum horizontal range: 15,500 yds
- Maximum vertical range: 37,000 ft
- Maximum effective ceiling: 30,000 ft

---

3 Pak is an abbreviation of "Panzerabwehrkanone" which means "anti-tank gun."

- Theoretical rate of fire: 25 rpm
- Practical rate of fire: 15 rpm
- Weight in action: 2.9 tons
- Elevation: -3° to +85°
- Traverse: 360°
- Length of barrel: 60 cals
- Weight of projectile: 14.3 lbs

i. 88-mm Dual-Purpose Gun (figs. 10 and 16)

(1) *Development.*—The German 8.8-cm gun was introduced in 1934 as the standard mobile AA gun. It was then known as the 8.8-cm Flak 18. In 1936, during the Spanish War, it proved a very effective weapon against tanks, which were at that time relatively lightly armored. In order to develop still further this dual-purpose employment, the Germans produced armor-piercing ammunition for the weapon, a telescopic sight suitable for the engagement of ground targets, and a more mobile carriage; an HE shell with a percussion fuse was also produced so that the weapon could, when necessary, be employed in a field-artillery role.

The improved equipment was ready in time for the Battle of France, when it proved itself capable of dealing with the heavier French tanks, against which the then standard AT gun, the 3.7-cm (1.45-in) Pak, was relatively ineffective. The next step was to provide the gun with a new carriage, from which the gun could engage tanks without being taken off its wheels, and to fit a shield. Still more recently, a self-propelled mount has been reported: and while there is no precise information as to its design, it appears that from this mount the gun can readily take on ground, but not air, targets.

(2) *Description.*—(a) *General.*—For all practical purposes, the operating characteristics of the 18, 36, and 38 models of this weapon are the same. The main characteristics of the 8.8-cm Flak 18 are as follows:
- Muzzle velocity: 2,755 f/s

- Maximum horizontal range: 16,600 yds
- Maximum vertical range: 35,700 ft
- Maximum effective ceiling: 34,770 ft
- Theoretical rate of fire: 25 rpm
- Practical rate of fire: 12 to 15 rpm
- Weight in action: 4.9 tons
- Weight in draft: 7.1 tons
- Elevation: -3° to +85°
- Traverse: 360° (limited to two complete revolutions of the handwheels, either side of zero, to avoid excessive twisting of the data transmission cable)
- Length of barrel: 56 cals

(b) *Gun data (8.8-cm Flak 18)*.—The gnu consists of a jacket, a sleeve, a removable tube in three sections, and a breech ring. The three-section tube is held in place by the breech ring in the rear and by a locking collar in the front, both of which are secured to the sleeve. The sleeve is secured to the jacket by a locking ring at the breech end. One of the joints in the three-section liner is the chamber of the gun and is therefore sealed by the shell case, but the other occurs at about one-third of the distance to the muzzle.

The breech mechanism is of the horizontal sliding-wedge type, semiautomatic, and self-cocking. As the gun recoils, the mechanism opens, ejects the empty case, and at the same time, compresses the striker and breechblock operating springs. Loading is by automatic rammer used in conjunction with a loading tray.

Firing is by percussion. The withdrawal of the loading tray will operate the firing mechanism unless set to "Hand." The breechblock may be opened and closed by hand if desired. The mechanism must be hand-operated for loading the first round. Safety arrangements are incorporated in the mechanism to prevent firing until the breech is in the closed position.

(c) *Mount data*.—The mount has a platform which rests

Figure 10.—8.8-cm (88-mm) dual-purpose gun in action.

squarely on the ground when the gun is in the firing position. The platform has four legs, with jacks at the outer ends of each for approximate leveling. In the traveling position, the two side legs fold upward. The pedestal is secured to the platform and supports the body through a gimbal ring and body pivot housing. The body, which contains the azimuth and elevation gears, supports the cradle on its trunnions and rotates in the housing for azimuth traverse. Accurate cross-leveling is accomplished by rocking the body pivot housing in the gimbal ring by means of cross-leveling handwheels on the platform. A 5-degree movement is possible by this means.

The gun slides on the cradle, to which it is connected through the recoil mechanism. The recoil system incorporates a hydraulic buffer below the barrel, and a hydro-pneumatic recuperator above. Both cylinders are secured to the cradle, and the pistons are connected to the breech ring. The buffer contains 18.8 pints of buffer fluid. The recuperator contains about 4 1/2 gallons of fluid and an approximately equal volume of air at 39 atmospheres. Length of recoil is variable, being about 1,050 mm at 0 degrees quadrant elevation, and 700 mm at 85 degrees quadrant elevation. The automatic rammer operates with the return cylinder, loading tray, and actuating mechanism. The internal construction of the return cylinder resembles that of the recuperator on a smaller scale.

A hand-operated fuze-setter with two openings is fitted to the left side of the body.

To put the gun in traveling position, the side legs are folded upward and secured. A limber and carriage are attached to the platform, which is raised by winches and secured. Some modifications of this gun are capable of being fired from the traveling position at ground targets, and there is also a model on a self-propelled mount.

(3) *Ammunition.*—The three types of ammunition used with this weapon are as follows:

Type	Weight of complete round	Length of complete round	Weight of projectile	Fuze
HE shell	31 lbs 11 1/2 oz	36.39 in	20 lbs 1 oz	Time-clockwork.
HE shell	32 lbs	36.69 in	20 lbs 5 oz	Nose percussion.
AP tracer	33 lbs	34.21 in	21 lbs 1/2 oz	Base.

Penetration of the AP projectile against homogeneous armor plate is show approximately on the table opposite.

(4) *Fire control.*—The gun may be laid on the target by three methods:

Range in yards	Thickness of plate	
	Normal	30°
1,000	4.7 in	4.1 in
1,500	4.2 in	3.7 in
2,000	3.7 in	3.1 in

(a) Indirect laying, by matching the pointers of the data receivers, which are controlled by the director (*Kommandogerät* No. 36, described in par. 8 b (1), below).

(b) Direct laying, by means of the Flak ZF 20–E telescopic sight. Vertical and lateral deflections are applied to the telescope, and the man at the azimuth handwheel puts the cross hairs on the target. The gun is elevated by the man on the elevation handwheel, who follows an indicating arm which moves with the sight.

(c) The dial sight may be used for laying the gun in azimuth, while the quadrant elevation is set in by the elevation man as ordered.

(5) *Mobility.*—This gun is normally towed by two types of half-track vehicles. These vehicles, which are respectively of 140 and 185 horsepower and weigh 11 1/2 and 14 1/2 tons loaded, carry the gun crew, as well as a supply of ammunition in lockers at the rear of the vehicle. The exact amount of ammunition carried is not known, but seems to be at least about 35 rounds.

(6) *Personnel.*—(a) *For action against aircraft.*—The gun detachment consists of a detachment commander and nine men, with duties for antiaircraft action as follows:
- Detachment Commander
- No. 1 : Elevation-setter
- No. 2 : Azimuth-setter
- No. 3 : Loading and firing number
- No. 4 : |
- No. 5 : | Ammunition numbers
- No. 6 : Fuze-setter
- No. 7 : |
- No. 8 : | Ammunition numbers

- No. 9 : |

(b) *For action against ground targets.*—For the engagement of ground targets, the duties of this gun detachment are as follows:
- Detachment Commander
- No. 1 : Elevation-setter
- No. 2 : Azimuth-setter
- No. 3 : Loading and firing number
- No. 4 : |
- No. 5 : | Ammunition numbers
- No. 6 : |
- No. 7 : |
- No. 8 : Range-setter
- No. 9 : Lateral-deflection setter

j. 105-mm AA Gun

(1) *Description.*—The 10.5-cm Flak 38 (4.14-inch) is being encountered in increasing numbers. Although the 8.8-cm gun, because of its success and in particular its value as a dual-purpose weapon, is likely to remain the main armament of heavy Flak, it is known that the 10.5-cm gun ranks high on German priorities for war production. The possibility that this larger weapon may be developed as an AA/AT gun must, therefore, be reckoned with. It is noteworthy that a new tractor-drawn mobile version was produced some time ago, although it is reported that the mount proved unsatisfactory.

Some of the main characteristics of this weapon are as follows:
- Muzzle velocity: 2,890 f/s
- Maximum horizontal range: 19,100 yds
- Maximum vertical range: 41,300 ft
- Maximum effective ceiling: 37,000 ft
- Theoretical rate of fire: 15 rpm
- Practical rate of fire: 8 to 10 rpm
- Weight in action: 11.56 tons
- Elevation: -3° to +87°

- Traverse: 360°
- Length of barrel: 60 cals
- Ammunition—three classes, as follows:

    (i) HE with time fuze (weight of projectile, 32 lbs 11 oz)

    (ii) HE with percussion fuze (weight of projectile, not known)

    (iii) AP with base fuze (weight of projectile, not known)

An automatic fuze-setter is used with the gun, but it is not known whether it operates on the same principles as does the fuze-setter fitted on the 8.8-cm weapon. Details of the loading and firing mechanism are not known, but they are probably substantially the same as for the 8.8-cm gun.

(2) *Fire control.*—The *Kommandogerät* No. 40 is employed with this gun for firing at aircraft. A description of the *Kommandogerät* No. 36, which is used with the 8.8-cm gun, is given in a later portion of this study (see par. 8b (1), below). It is believed that the No. 40 operates on the same principle as the No. 36. In addition, the *Kommandohilfsgerät* No. 35 (auxiliary predictor) can also be used with this gun. A description of the latter instrument appears elsewhere in this study.

(3) *Personnel.*—Except for additional men that might be required to handle the heavier ammunition, the personnel comprising the gun detachment is substantially the same as for the 8.8-cm weapon.

k. 127-mm AA Gun

The 12.7-cm Flak 38 (5-inch) is a naval AA weapon. Although this gun is known to be used by the Germans, mainly in a static AA role in Germany, little reliable data is available concerning its characteristics and operation. Its known main characteristics are as follows:

- Muzzle velocity: 2,500 f/s
- Maximum horizontal range: 19,600 yds
- Maximum vertical range: 42,600 ft
- Maximum effective ceiling: 35,000 to 40,000 ft

- Theoretical rate of fire: 12 rpm
- Practical rate of fire: 8 rpm
- Elevation: 0° to 90°
- Traverse: 360°
- Weight of projectile: 55 lbs
- Length of barrel: 50 cals

l. 150-mm AA Gun

The 15-cm Flak 39 (5.91-inch) is used by the Germans in a dual-purpose role, for AA and coast defense. For the most part it is found on fixed mounts in static roles, manned to a large extent by Navy personnel. Little accurate information is available on this gun, but the following limited data will serve to give some indication of its capabilities:[4]

- Muzzle velocity: 3,450 f/s
- Maximum horizontal range: 34,000 yds
- Maximum vertical range: 66,000 ft
- Maximum effective ceiling: 40,000 to 45,000 ft
- Theoretical rate of fire: 12 rpm
- Practical rate of fire: 6 to 8 rpm
- Weight of projectile: 88.6 lbs

8. Fire Control

a. Solution of the AA Fire-Control Problem

There is no indication that a director of any type is ordinarily used with the light and medium Flak guns, the Germans apparently having decided that the development of the Flak sights already described is more profitable and practicable than the development of directors. For use with heavy guns. the German development of fire-control apparatus is strikingly similar to our own. They have an older, angular-speed director which is used for auxiliary purposes, but the latest and most commonly used instrument operates on the linear-speed method, using present azimuth, present angular height, and present slant range as basic elements.

---

4 The data is from German sources and cannot be adequately verified.

b. Equipment

(1) *Kommandogerät (stereoscopic fire director)* (figs. 11 and 12).—(a) *Description.*—This fire-control instrument combines into one instrument a 4-meter-base Zeiss stereoscopic height- and range-finder, and a director. Two types are known: the No. 36, employed with the 8.8-cm Flak gun, and the No. 40, employed with the 10.5-cm Flak gun. The principles and method of operation of the No. 40 are not known, but they are probably similar to those of the No. 36, details of which follow.

(b) *Method of operation.*—The stages in the production of the firing data in the No. 36 are as follows:

(1) The height- and range-finder furnishes present azimuth, angle of sight, and slant range to the target, all of which may be termed initial data.

(2) The rate of change, obtained by continuously feeding this data into the predictor, provides the horizontal ground speed and the course angle of the target, which may be termed intermediate data.

(Note that the range-finder is carried separately.)

(3) The combination of initial and intermediate data provides the vertical and lateral defection and range correction to determine the future position. From this combination, the gun data is obtained by mechanical computation within the

Figure 11.—Kommandogerät in traveling position.

Figure 12.—Kommandogerät ready for use.

predictor.

(c) *Transmission of data to guns.*—The gun data thus obtained (in terms of firing azimuth, quadrant elevation, and fuze) are normally transmitted electrically to the guns, in the following manner: each of the three receiver dials at the gun (i.e., for firing azimuth, quadrant elevation, and fuze) is provided with three mechanical pointers pivoted at the center of the dial. There are three concentric circles on the dial, each with 10 holes numbered from 0 to 9, each hole being fitted with an electric bulb. The outer circle represents units; the center, tens; and the inner, hundreds. The appropriate bulbs light up in accordance with the data transmitted from the *Kommandogerät*. The actual value of the reading is different for each dial, the unit (i.e., on the outer circle) in each instance having the following values:

- Azimuth receiver : 0.36°
- Elevation receiver : 0.10°
- Fuze receiver : 0.5 (of the German system of fuze range)[5]

These figures provide a measure of the limits of accuracy obtained in transmission. The two gun-layers and the fuze-setter bring their mechanical data pointers into coincidence (covering

---

5 The German fuze scale reads from 0 to 350, the numerals being reference numbers which indicate definite times of flight.

the illuminated bulbs with the transparent celluloid ends of the pointers) by manually actuating azimuth and elevation handwheels on the guns, and the fuze-setting handwheel on the machine fuze-setter.

(2) *Kommandohilfsgerät (auxiliary fire director).*—This instrument is used for auxiliary purposes, and operates on the principle of calculation of the rates of change of angular velocity. A separate 4-meter-base stereoscopic height- and range-finder provides the present slant range to the target, and this data is passed orally to the director. By following the target continuously for azimuth and elevation, and by setting in range continuously, the rates of change of azimuth, elevation, and slant range are obtained. These, multiplied by time of flight, give the lateral and vertical deflections and a correction for range. These corrections, applied to the present data, provide future data which are corrected for abnormal ballistic conditions, dead time, and drift, and which are then passed to the guns as gun azimuth, quadrant elevation, and fuze. Data in this case are transmitted to the guns by telephone, no electrical transmission being provided.

(3) *Telescopic sight for 88-mm gun.*—The 8.8-cm gun is fitted with a telescopic sight primarily for the engagement of ground targets; the latest type is the telescopic sight 20-E (ZF 20-E). It weighs about 10 pounds and is a monocular type with a magnification of four and a field view of 17.5 degrees. The reticle is made with two cross lines interrupted at the center to form a laying mark, an arrangement which is usual in German instruments. There is a range drum graduated in hundreds from 0 to 9,400 meters, and a super-elevation drum with graduations of 1/16 of a degree, from 0° to 12°. There are also lateral- and vertical-deflection drums.

For AT use, the lateral- and vertical-deflection drums are set to zero. Range is set on the range drum, thereby automatically applying the necessary super-elevation. Corrections from observation of fire are applied to deflection drums as required.

An older type of instrument, the 2F 20, may be fitted. This has the same particulars, but no range drum; superelevation must be found from a range table and applied.

(4) *Radio-location equipment.*—It is known that German radio-location equipment for fire-control data is being produced on a high priority, and there is no doubt that this will constitute a most important line of future development. This activity is taking place parallel to the development of radio-detection equipment for warning against hostile aircraft. Aerial observers flying over gun positions in Germany and the gun-defended portions of occupied European countries have reported seeing instruments, identified as German radio-location instruments, in close proximity to gun positions. This would indicate that these radio-location instruments are being used with gun batteries, probably as a means of furnishing early basic data to the directors. Another possible use of these instruments is to furnish early information for calculation of data for barrage and deterrent fire.

9. Searchlights

a. Heavy Searchlights

(1) Equipment.—*(a) General.*—The equipment used with a heavy searchlight consists of four main units: a sound locator, the searchlight, an optical director, and the generator. Beyond the introduction of remote control, little is known of recent developments in German searchlight equipment. Some searchlights of 200-cm, or larger, diameter have been developed, and the sound locator has possibly been improved by the introduction of some form of electrical amplification. The standard heavy searchlight, however, is the 150-cm (60–inch) size. Information from radio-location equipment is almost certainly passed to the searchlights, but the extent and method of its application are unknown.

(b) The ring-trumpet sound locator derives its name from

the construction of the four trumpets or horns as a single unit of ring shape. Ordinary stethoscopic listening by two listeners, one for azimuth and one for elevation, is employed. The base length is 135 cm (53.1 inches), giving a theoretical accuracy of about one-half degree. In average weather conditions, the range is about 6,600 yards. The trumpets can be moved through 360° in azimuth and from 0° to 108° in elevation. The "lag calculator" is in the base of the sound locator. Estimated target and sound speeds (the latter based on weather conditions) are set into the lag calculator, which continuously reconstructs the triangle formed by the line of sound reception, the line of sight (present position), and the target course. The azimuth and elevation of the line of sight are shown electrically both at the sound locator and at the searchlight. The sound locator and the searchlight are connected by a cable.

(c) The 150-cm (60-inch) searchlight (fig. 13) has a glass parabolic reflector of 150-cm diameter. The focal length is 650 mm. The high-current-density arc lamp is self-regulating and is fitted in an inverted position in the projector barrel. The light is of 990 million candle power and has a range in favorable weather of 8,800 yards at a height of 13,000 to 16,500 feet. The current consumption is 200 amperes at 77 volts. The projector can be moved in azimuth through 360°, and in elevation from -12° through the vertical to -12° on the other side. The movement of the projector in azimuth is by means of a control arm, which is normally manipulated by hand; its movement in elevation is by means of either of two handwheels, one on the control arm and one on the opposite side of the projector. Electrical receivers for azimuth and elevation show the azimuth and elevation of the line of sight calculated by the sound locator. The beam is exposed and covered by a shutter of Venetian-blind type. More recent models are believed to be equipped with azimuth and elevation driving-motors which can be operated by automatic remote control from the sound locator or from the optical

Figure 13.—150-cm (60-inch) standard searchlight.

director; the exposing and covering of the beam on these models is controlled from the optical director. It is understood that the driving motors have three or four speeds, 1 degree and/or 1.5, 4, and 16 degrees per second.

(The elevation receiver is on the side of the drum near the extended hand control, and the azimuth receiver is in the rear.)

(d) The optical director consists of a pair of night glasses of ample magnification mounted on a tripod. The director is fitted with an overhead, open sight and with scales showing the azimuth and elevation to which the night glasses are pointing. When employed with remote-control equipment, it is believed that the optical director is located 30 to 45 yards from the searchlight, thus becoming in effect a control station.

(e) The searchlight generator is driven by an 8-cylinder internal-combustion engine which develops 51 horsepower at 1,500 revolutions per minute. The 24-kilowatt generator gives a direct current of 200 amperes at 110 volts at 1,500 revolutions per minute. The cable to the searchlight projector is 220 yards long.

(2) Mobility.—The sound locator, searchlight, and generator are each mounted on a detachable four-wheeled trailer of standard pattern, towed by a truck. Each section or unit therefore requires three trucks for transportation purposes.

(3) Personnel.—The individual searchlight section is composed of 14 individuals with duties as follows:
- Section Commander
- No. 1 : Searchlight layer for elevation
- No. 2 : Searchlight controller and layer for azimuth
- No. 3 : Lamp attendant
- No. 4 : Optical director spotter
- No. 5 : Generator attendant
- No. 6 : Engine attendant
- No. 7 : Lag-calculator operator
- No. 8 : Azimuth listener
- No. 9 : Elevation listener
- No. 10 : Sound locator spotter
- 3 truck drivers

(4) Communications.—Field telephones are the normal means of communication, each battery having three telephone-erection parties, with sufficient equipment to connect the searchlight sections to platoon headquarters, which, in turn, are connected to battery headquarters. Communications with battalion headquarters are also normally by telephone. Each battery has one small truck equipped with voice radio for communication with the battalion, and two details with pack voice-radio for use within the battery as required.

b. Light Searchlights

(1) Equipment.—*(a) General.*—The equipment consists of a 60-cm (23.50-inch) searchlight and a generator. This highly mobile and easily handled equipment, designed for use without

a sound locator against low-flying targets, appears to have given satisfaction in the limited role for which it was intended. There are no indications that any changes in the design are contemplated.

(b) The 60-cm (23.58-inch) searchlight has a glass parabolic reflector of 60-cm diameter. The focal length is 250 mm. The high-current-density arc lamp is self-regulating and is fitted in an inverted position in the projector barrel. The light is of 135 million candle power and has a range (in focus) in favorable weather of 5,700 yards at a height of 5,000 feet; with dispersed beam the range is 3,500 yards. The current consumption is 90 amperes at 60 volts. The projector is moved in azimuth and elevation by handwheels operated by the searchlight controller, who is seated behind the projector barrel. The beam is exposed and covered by a shutter of Venetian-blind type.

(c) An 8-kilowatt searchlight generator gives the required current at 85 volts. It is connected to the searchlight by a cable 110 yards long.

(2) Mobility.—The projector is mounted on a detachable two-wheeled trailer, towed by a truck. The same truck carries the generator, which can either be operated in the body of the truck or be unloaded on the ground.

(3) Personnel.—The individual searchlight section is composed of five individuals with duties as follows:
- Section Commander
- No. 1 : Searchlight controller
- No. 2 : Lamp attendant
- No. 3 : Generator attendant
- Truck driver

No. 1 lays the searchlight as ordered, and puts the light into action with a dispersed beam. The section commander gives directional orders and orders a search, if required. The search is carried out in S-shape light-tracks across the target course. If No. 1 gets on target, No. 2 puts the beam in focus. No. 1 shuts off the beam on the section commander's orders.

(4) Communications.—Since light searchlights normally operate directly with light-gun platoons, the light-searchlight section from the communication point of view is normally serviced by the light Flak battery or platoon with which the light-searchlight section is operating.

10. Barrage Balloons

a. General

Although no extensive use of barrage balloons was contemplated by the Germans before the beginning of World War II, subsequent developments proved that barrage balloons have a definite psychological value as well as a practical value, and experiments conducted prior to the outbreak of the war were very soon put into practical use over strategic manufacturing centers in western Germany.

As in the U.S. Army and in the British Isles, the main purpose of the German barrage balloon is to hold a steel cable suspended vertically in the air. Thus, below the operating height of the balloon, this cable obstacle presents both a physical and mental hazard to enemy pilots attempting to enter that space. It is of course axiomatic that the type of balloon used for this purpose will be strong enough to suspend the cable, and that the balloon is designed in accordance with sound aeronautical principles (i.e., in terms of streamlining, capacity to resist wind stress, etc.). The extent of engineering developments of the German barrage balloon since the beginning of World War II is not definitely known, but it is believed that any changes effected consist only of minor modifications of the types in existence at the beginning of the war.

b. Description (fig. 14)

At the beginning of World War II, there were two general types of barrage balloons in existence in Germany. Both types were egg-shaped and had four fins at the tail end: a top fin, two side fins, and a bottom fin. The top fin and two side fins were inflated with air.

Figure 14.—German barrage balloon.

The bottom fin was called the steering sack and had an opening at both ends. When the balloon was up, air entered the bottom opening of the fin and made its exit through the top opening. The fins (and especially the bottom fin) served to keep the balloon in proper position with respect to the wind and air currents. When inflated, the shape of the balloon could be likened to a short fat cigar, with a tail like a Japanese goldfish. Rubber cords were fastened tightly around the outside of the inflated balloon to assist in keeping its shape and strength.

Although both types of balloons were inflated with hydrogen gas, they differed in that one type was inflated exclusively with hydrogen gas while the second was inflated with both hydrogen gas and air, each being in separate chambers. At least the first type, and probably both types, were divided into six gas chambers. The second type had its air compartment behind the hydrogen gas compartment, the air being forced out through air valves as the gas expanded at higher altitudes. As both types were still more or less in the experimental stage, they varied in size, the largest being approximately 60 feet long and 25 feet in diameter, with a long "flutter" tail. Although various types of lethal devices were in the process of experimentation, the final decision along these lines is not known.

SECTION III. USE OF AA WITH FIELD FORCES

11. Introduction

A discussion of the war-time use of AA artillery by the Germans falls into two general classifications: use with the field forces and use in defense of Germany and other static rear-area objectives. In this classification, however, it should be remembered that German tactical doctrine holds that organizations and weapons should not be placed in a purely defensive role except where the tactical situation absolutely demands such disposition. Wherever possible, an offensive plan will always take precedence over a plan which is purely defensive. Thus, even in rear-area and static positions, the German commander will, insofar as possible, build up his plan of organization and action in such manner as to incorporate as much of the offensive theory of operation as the situation will permit. This general underlying principle of German employment of troops and materiel should always be kept in mind in connection with the following discussion, which in accordance with the above classification has been divided into a section covering the use of AA with forces in the field and a section covering the use of AA in Germany and other static defense areas.

12. General Principles

a. The German Task Force

A German general has stated that the real secret of the initial success of the German Arms was "the combined employment of all arms on the battlefield in pursuance of one common mission." Related to this statement is the German conception of a task force as a grouping of the necessary arms and services, under one commander, for the accomplishment of a definite specified mission. Use of the task force implements another basic principle of command: that for a given mission a commander is selected, given the means, and allowed to carry out the assignment unhampered.

b. Antiaircraft Task Force Allocation

Following the general principle, AA artillery is assigned to specific task forces by the German High Command in accordance with the estimated need for AA artillery in execution of the mission. The size and composition of the AA artillery units so assigned will depend on several considerations, the most important of which are as follows:

- The mission (and its importance);
- The amount and characteristics of enemy aviation;
- The amount, types, and characteristics of friendly aviation available;
- The commander's estimate of the means required;
- The amount and type of AA artillery materiel available;
- The terrain;
- Proximity to the enemy;
- The weather and the season of the year.

c. Primary Missions of AA

In general, the primary missions of the AA artillery are considered by the Germans to be as follows:

- Defense against hostile aerial reconnaissance;
- Defense against hostile artillery observation;
- Defense against hostile air attacks on personnel and important installations;
- Support of friendly air combat strength.

Light, medium, and heavy AA weapons supplement each other in their effect. While the light and medium AA weapons furnish protection against low-flying hostile aircraft, the heavy weapons bear the brunt of the AA defense in the combat zone, combining long range with rapid fire and mobility.

The main mission of the heavy AA guns is to protect the ground against air reconnaissance and high-altitude attacks while on the march, at rest, or in actual combat. Moved by tractor or truck, the average marching speed of these heavy AA guns is from 5 to

20 miles per hour. Horse-drawn AA cannon are employed only by units contending with fuel shortages or very unsuitable road nets. Antiaircraft units moved by tractor or truck can be prepared for action rapidly; they have great mobility, and can be employed within the effective range of hostile artillery.

d. Transition from AA Role to Other Roles

In the approach to battle, as contact is made with the enemy, the German task force commander will utilize all facilities under his control to gain control of the air. For this purpose, he will employ all the aircraft at his disposal. During this same phase AA artillery will be employed in its primary mission of ground defense against hostile aircraft.

As control of the air is achieved, there is a transition in the employment of the ground arms. In direct proportion to the completeness achieved in control of the air, AA artillery becomes available for other missions. Since AA artillery guns combine the advantages of high mobility, high muzzle-velocity, accurate and rapid firing methods, and a flat trajectory, they are used against tanks and armored vehicles once their need in an AA role has become secondary.

While acting in their primary role, AA weapons will be employed against tanks, armored vehicles, or other ground targets only as a means of self-defense, or under circumstances where principles of surprise fire may apply. Since AA artillery is used by the Germans quite extensively to protect field artillery installations against hostile aircraft during the early phase when air control is being established, AA units in performance of this mission often find themselves in forward areas, and their very existence frequently depends on the ability to engage hostile tanks and armored vehicles.

Experiments with the use of AA guns (especially the 88-mm in the Spanish Civil War), together with later practical experiences in the Battle of France, resulted in AA weapons being mounted so that they could be used against ground as well as air targets. The

88-mm gun is the best example of this development, and its use in Russia against heavily armored vehicles was so successful that it began to be used more and more in a separate antitank role. This role has received much publicity and attention, but it should not obscure the fact that on most occasions the primary mission of the 88-mm gun is against hostile aircraft.

13. Operational Use Against Air Targets

a. General

It is a frequently repeated axiom in the German Army that every combat unit is responsible for its own AA defense against low-flying aircraft. Every man armed with a rifle is trained to use it against such aerial targets, it having been found that concentrated fire by rifles is very effective against attack by low-flying or strafing planes, up to slant ranges of about 500 yards. Machine-gun fire is considered effective up to about 800 yards; light- and medium-caliber AA cannon, up to a slant range of about 2,000 yards. Heavy AA artillery is considered as being effective for fire up to about 9,000 yards, but is not generally considered as being available for use against planes flying directly over the battery at altitudes of less than 400 yards. For this reason each heavy battery is supported by two 20-mm AA cannon, which are an organic part of the battery organization. Figure 15, which is taken from an authoritative German military manual used extensively by German junior officers, gives an analysis of the slant ranges of responsibility for defense against enemy aerial targets. It should be noted, however, that the maximum slant ranges shown in the figure are less than the actual maximum capacities of the weapons concerned.

b. Protection of Columns on the March

(1) *Panzer divisions.*—German Panzer divisions on the move are trained to keep a considerable distance between separate units and groups, and where possible the division generally marches in several columns along parallel roads. Usually the majority

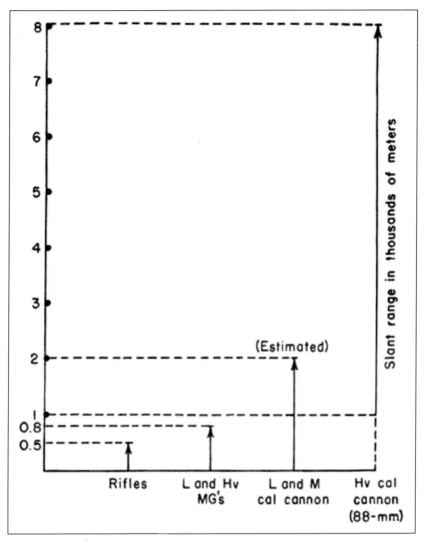

Figure 15.—Slant-range chart.

of AA guns will be found well forward in the columns, and all defiles, bridges, and stopping places will be well defended by AA units. The columns usually halt after 2 hours for 20 minutes' rest, and after 4 or 5 hours' movement a halt of at least 3 hours is normal.

In the event of air attack, the column continues its march, and machine guns and the light and medium AA gun crews open fire. If the air attack proves to be of such weight that casualties to truck-borne troops will be severe, the column halts and the troops take cover. The drivers, however, remain with their vehicles. When air attack threatens in open country, the tank columns deploy in open formation, usually V-shaped.

(2) *Other units.*—As mentioned above, all German troops are trained to use their rifles and machine guns for mass fire-power against low-flying and strafing airplanes, while on the march as well as in other situations. Antiaircraft artillery units, both organic *Heeresflak* units and attached Luftwaffe AA units, furnish the necessary AA protection in essentially the same manner as when operating with armored divisions, the only difference being that slower-moving units and supply echelons may require a special type of defense. It should also be remembered that, in cases Where the AA artillery is defending supply echelons, AA emplacements along prescribed routes of supply may be more or less static in nature.

c. Use in Forward Areas with Attacking Units

(1) *General.*—The use of AA units attached to Army divisions and corps will vary with the situation and in accordance with the higher commander's views as to how the AA artillery under his control can best be used in carrying out his attack mission.

(2) *Example of use with an attacking Panzer division.*—An order of the 15th Panzer Division, dated May 25, 1942, gives an interesting insight into the divisional commander's employment of the AA forces at his disposal. The order is for the assembly of the division in preparation for an attack. The 15th Panzer Division occupied a central position, the 90th Light Division being on the right and the 21st Panzer Division on the left. The 15th Panzer Division was organized into four groups as follows: an armored group, a reconnaissance group, a supporting group, and an infantry group mounted on trucks.

(a) *Disposition of AA forces.*—The AA forces at the disposal of the 15th Panzer Division by this order consisted of—

(1) An AA battalion staff;

(2) One heavy AA battery (6 heavy and 2 light guns),

(3) One light AA battery (12 light guns), Luftwaffe

(4) One light AA battery, less one section (9 light guns); AA troops

(5) One AA company (12 light guns) of organic *Heeresflak* troops.

These forces were distributed as follows:

	Allocated to
(1) AA battalion staff	Staff of 15th Pz Div (in the supporting group).
(2) Heavy AA battery	8th Tk Regt (in the armored group). Prior to the commencement of the operation, the heavy AA battery was ordered to protect the assembly against air attack.
(3) Light AA Battery (12 light guns):	
Battery staff and 1 section (3 light guns).	Field artillery and engineers of the armored group.
One section (3 light guns).	Field artillery of the supporting group.
One section (3 light guns).	Heavy AA battery ((2) above) for local defense against low-flying aircraft.
(4) Light AA battery, less 1 section (9 light guns):	
Battery staff and 1 section (3 light guns).	AA battalion staff (in the supporting group).
One section (3 light guns).	Engineers of the supporting group.
One section (3 light guns).	Staff of the 15th Pz Div.
(5) AA Company (12 light guns):	
Company staff and 2 sections (8 light guns).	Mounted infantry group.
One section (4 light guns).	Reconnaissance group.

(b) *Analysis of dispositions.*—The following points of interest arise from an analysis of the order and the above dispositions:

(1) The chain of command is from the AA battalion staff (attached to the staff of the Panzer division), through the heavy and light battery staffs with the armored group and the light battery staff with the support group.

(2) The heavy battery is seen in a dual role. In the approach to battle it provides AA protection; it turns to the ground role in support of the tanks when battle is joined.

(3) The light batteries protect the divisional and AA battery staffs, the field artillery, the engineers, and the heavy AA battery against low-flying attack. The ground role is secondary.

(4) The organic AA company gives protection against low-flying attack to the mounted infantry and reconnaissance groups.

(5) The forces mentioned in the orders of the 15th Panzer

Division do not comprise an entire mixed AA battalion, the missing elements being two heavy batteries and one section of a light battery. In this connection, it is known that a considerable force of heavy AA guns (no doubt accompanied by a few light guns for close protection) was operating as an independent antitank group in this operation, and the missing elements of the battalion were undoubtedly assigned to the separate ground-target mission.

d. Protection of Rear-Area Installations

In operating with task forces, certain of the attached AA units are allotted for protection of Army and Air Force installations. Even in moving situations, AA must be designated to defend important semipermanent installations such as depots, parks, railheads, bridges, airdromes, etc. No hard-and-fast set rule is laid down for this use of AA artillery. The size of the AA force defending such areas will depend to a large extent on the AA artillery which is available for this assignment. Another consideration is whether or not superiority of air power has been attained.

Employment of the available AA forces will vary. In the western campaign in May, 1940, the AA defense of the German forces in the main attack over the Meuse River from Dinant to Sedan remained in the hands of an AA corps commander. The AA corps was composed of a number of AA divisions, each organized into regiments and separate battalions. Once the crossing was affected, the AA units comprising the corps were attached to other forces advancing on their missions. In later stages of that campaign, it was customary for the AA artillery to protect forward elements by attaching one battalion of three 88–mm gun batteries to each army corps, and one battalion of the same size to each army.

e. Defense of Railway Trains

(1) *General.*—The mounting of AA materiel on railway mounts for the protection of railway trains and as a means of furnishing a mobile defense of lines of communication has been highly perfected by the Germans. It should be noted that AA guns

mounted on railway mounts can be used either in rear areas for protection of trains operating therein, or for the protection of trains carrying troops or supplies to forward combat areas. For example, the Germans use these mounts for the protection of important trains operating in Germany, but they also have had these mounts in large numbers throughout Russia during the Russian Campaign. Although the 20-mm Flak single- or four-barreled gun is normally employed, it is known that the 37-mm, the 88-mm, 105-mm, and possibly the 75-mm and 150-mm Flak guns are also used for this purpose.

(2) *Method.*—A German manual lays down certain rules for employment of AA guns on railway mounts. A flatcar known as the *R-Wagen* is the truck prescribed by the German manual for use with the 20-mm gun. The gun is mounted on one end of the car. The crew is carried under a removable roof on the other end. Safe defenses are put up around the gun for "safe" firing zones. The manual prescribes three general methods in which protection may be given to trains:

- Three cars mounted with a machine gun on AA mounts and situated respectively one-fourth, one-half, and three-fourths of the way along the train;
- Three trucks carrying 20-mm light Flak guns, one in the middle of the train, one at the rear, and one immediately behind the locomotive. The gun behind the locomotive is usually not manned, being a spare to permit reversing the train without shunting the guns.

On especially important trains an additional 20-mm gun may be carried on a truck in front of the locomotive.

On the move, the guns are continuously manned, priority areas of 180 degrees being allotted as follows:

- Forward: To the front machine gun and the center 20-mm Flak guns;
- Rearward: To the center and rear machine guns, and the rear 20-mm Flak guns;

- Forward: To the 20-mm Flak gun (when carried) in front of the locomotive.

These means of defense of railway trains are not necessarily the only ones possible, as it is known that the position (or sequence of the positions) of AA guns protecting the trains may be changed at any time to comply with particular requirements.

Since care must be taken that the AA guns are not struck by obstructions such as passing trains, tunnels, signal posts, etc., lookouts are detailed to observe on each side of the train. When not firing, the 20-mm guns are pointed directly to the front or rear depending on their sector of fire.

Since no warning of attacks can be expected, all AA personnel must be kept in a constant state of readiness. There are two aircraft watchers, one observing an arc of 180 degrees to the front, the other to the rear. These watchers are selected from among the best-trained men and relieved frequently.

When the train is moving, where possible only tracer ammunition is used, since the motion does not permit accurate sighting. Care is taken not to shoot up signal posts and other installations, and where there are overhead powerlines, no firing is done even under attack.

f. Searchlights

Searchlight units consisting of heavy searchlights are normally assigned to task forces only in those cases where the assigned mission may require their use. With field forces engaged in offensive operations, the employment of heavy searchlights will be rare. Their use would normally be confined to rear areas, under circumstances where the situation has become static and it is necessary to employ heavy AA protection. Inasmuch as light searchlights are an organic part of the light AA battalions, a certain number of light searchlight batteries will be found moving into forward areas with the field forces. As their use will be limited, however, the tendency of German commanders is to leave the bulk of the searchlights in rear-area positions for defense of those areas.

As these light searchlight batteries are highly mobile, it should be remembered that the commander can also use them in a variety of ways other than against aircraft, such as defense against parachute troops and in night ground attacks.

g. Antiaircraft Warning System

For warning against hostile aircraft both in the field and in rear areas, the Germans have a troop-warning service of the AA artillery which is similar in principle to the Antiaircraft Artillery Information Service (AAAIS) of U.S. AA units. Every active German AA unit observes the air in the area under its jurisdiction with specially trained personnel known as air guards. Through a system of communication facilities, these air guards submit detailed reports of hostile aircraft in their vicinity. Under normal circumstances the AA battalion headquarters is responsible for forwarding appropriate warning reports to the air-arm commander at higher headquarters.

14. Operational Use Against Ground Targets

a. General

The basic principle of German combat methods has been said to be a clever adaptation of fire to movement, with fire power increasing directly in proportion to the resistance encountered. Movement is normally from one piece of advantageous terrain to another, with maximum fire applied during the movement. Both fire and movement are applied with one basic purpose in view: to attain the objective of the unit. This principle is applicable to the offensive combat of all German units, from squads to armies.

In defense the German commander chooses the most suitable ground for combined action by infantry, machine guns, antitank guns, artillery, and tanks. In such depth as resources permit, he will usually construct a series of defense areas capable of all-around defense against any form of attack. The artillery of all types will be placed where it can support either the defense area, or the tanks if these are launched in a counterattack. In withdrawals, after skillfully thinning our most of the transport facilities and battle impedimenta, the German commander will usually launch some form of feint action to cover the withdrawal of the remainder of the force. This feint action often takes place in the evening; during the night the whole force withdraws, leaving only reconnaissance elements supported by a few guns to hold up hostile forces. In any of the above general situations, full use in roles against ground targets can be expected to be made of any AA guns not specifically required for use in an AA role.

b. 88-mm Dual-Purpose Gun

(1) *In antitank roles.*—Using both HE and AP ammunition, the 88-mm Flak gun has been used on all fronts with deadly effect against medium and heavy tanks. Its worth as an AT weapon was proved in the Polish and French campaigns; since the beginning of the Russian Campaign, when it was used with much success against large Russian tanks the armor of which proved invulnerable to the then standard German 37-mm AT gun, the 88-mm gun has been considered by the Germans to be their heavy AT weapon.

Wherever balanced AT support is considered necessary, it is now considered usual for German task-force commanders to allot a certain proportion of 88-mm guns for purely AT roles. This is especially true since the weapon has made its appearance on the new 12-ton half-track vehicle, which is armored in front and carries a small supply of ammunition. When mounted on this self-propelled mount, the gun is used only for engaging ground targets, necessary AA protection being furnished from other sources. It should be remembered, however, that the gun can also be used in an AT role when mounted on the special trailer (No. 201), which is fitted with pneumatic tires and is drawn by a half-track vehicle carrying the gun crew and a small supply of ammunition. Such ground targets as tanks can be engaged while the gun is in this traveling position.

(2) *In other roles.*—Since German military commanders are

trained to utilize all available weapons to a maximum degree, it is not at all surprising that this gun has been used in other than AA and AT roles. Thus, in the battle for Sevastopol in the Russian Campaign, the German command was confronted with a narrow front barricaded completely with concrete, steel, and guns. In view of the mobility of the 88-mm Flak gun, an AA combat detachment manning one of these guns was ordered to support a local infantry attack. At short ranges and over open sights, this gun engaged pillboxes and other enemy centers of resistance which the infantry could not overcome, thus assisting the infantry in carrying out its mission.

In many sectors, this gun has been used in normal field artillery roles. It has been used against fortified bunkers as well as against personnel. In the crossing of the Albert Canal in the Western Campaign, it was used in a ground role to cover the bridging operations being carried on by engineers.

(3) *Fire-control methods.*—For use against armored vehicles, and for field artillery tasks, the following four methods of fire control have been used: direct fire, using a telescopic sight; director control; fire directed from an observation post; and air burst HE.

(a) *Direct fire.*—This has been the most successful method employed against armored vehicles. Apart from the extreme mobility of the gun, the efficient telescopic sight has contributed largely to the success of the 88-mm gun in an AT role. The latest mark of telescopic sight used is the ZF 20-E, which has already been described.

(b) *Director control.*—With director control, the data for the first round is calculated in the same manner as for an air target. Corrections for direction, range, and fuze range are made from observation of fire and arbitrarily set into the director. This method has not proved very satisfactory.

(c) *Fire directed from an OP.*—When the target is below the horizontal, or at ranges greater than 10,340 yards (i.e., beyond the limit of the telescopic sight), fire may be directed from an observation post. The OP officer takes azimuth, range, and elevation from his fire-control map. From these, he calculates the firing data with a range table and transmits the data to the gun position by telephone. A director is sometimes used for giving the initial direction to the guns. Corrections are ordered from observation of fire and are applied at the guns.

(d) *Air-burst HE.*—Fire for effect with time-fuze air-burst HE against troops in the open, and against battery positions, has also been reported. Ranging is carried out with a low height of burst. Fire for effect follows with the fuze range being adjusted to obtain the most effective height of burst. It is believed that this method is not used very often.

c. Light and Medium Flak Guns

(1) *In an antitank role.*—The light- and medium-caliber Flak guns (20-mm and 37-mm) have had less outstanding success against tanks and armored vehicles than has the 88-mm, owing undoubtedly to the fact that the smaller caliber somewhat limits their use. However, there is no question that with their extreme mobility and high rate of fire, and the penetrating effect of their AP shells, the smaller guns will continue to be used extensively in AT roles, particularly in emergencies.

(2) *In other roles.*—Aside from AT roles, light flak weapons, particularly the 20-mm, have been used for many different purposes against ground targets. They have been used against hostile machinegun nests, and bunkers have been neutralized by using these weapons for attacks on the openings. They have been employed in occupied villages and towns to overcome scattered resistance, and, like the 88-mm guns, they have also given ground support to engineers engaged in bridging operations.

(3) *General.*—Fire control for all the above uses is by normal or telescopic sight, with observation of the tracer.

15. Establishment of Gun Positions
a. Heavy AA Guns
(1) *For primary AA role.*—In the normal battery of four heavy AA guns, the pieces are disposed roughly in a square of approximately 70 yards. A fully equipped battery position will have two command posts, but this may vary in accordance with the importance of the locality and the availability of fire-control equipment. There are also several types of six-gun layouts.

(2) *For other roles.*—Emplacement of the 88-mm gun when being used primarily against tanks or in a role other than AA depends partly upon the terrain and partly upon certain rules laid down for the selection of a firing position, as follows: the angle of impact should not be greater than 60 degrees; the range should generally not exceed 2,000 yards; the gun level should slope downward (since the gun level varies from -3° to +15° from the horizontal of the muzzle); the position should be concealed, and as near to the target as possible in order to insure maximum accuracy and surprise in opening fire; the lanes of approach and withdrawal must be as firm, level, and wide as possible.

As both the four- and six-gun layouts used in forward areas do not differ materially from those prescribed for AA guns engaged in the defense of Germany and in other static rear-area positions, attention is invited to the discussion of this subject appearing in Section IV of this study.

b. Light and Medium AA Guns
Light and medium Flak guns are normally disposed in platoons of three. A triangular layout is common but not unchangeable, with the guns anywhere from 75 to 150 yards apart. These light guns are seldom deployed singly; however, in other than AA roles their use may depend primarily on emergency conditions, with consequent deviations from normal methods of disposition.

16. Deception and Concealment
Common German practice in all types of military operations, as

enunciated in their field service regulations, calls for the maximum use of surprise, which in turn involves secrecy, deception, and speed of execution. During the early European campaigns of the present war, because of overwhelming initial aerial superiority, the Germans did not pay too much attention to the camouflage of AA positions and to other passive defense practices. In later and present campaigns, however, the Germans have not always had definite air superiority, and they have used many passive means of deception and concealment, such as camouflage and erection of dummy gun positions and objectives, to protect themselves from aerial observation and to assist in maintaining the secrecy of their dispositions and operations. In the Libyan Desert, much ingenuity has been shown in concealing AA weapons, especially through dummy gun positions. Vehicles as well as guns are camouflaged with nets and local material, and resort is had to as much dispersion as possible under the tactical circumstances. In one operation in July of 1941, German guns were located among abandoned Italian artillery which had been left there from previous battles. These guns were not noticed until they opened fire.[6]

SECTION IV. USE OF AA IN DEFENSE OF GERMANY AND REAR AREAS

17. Historical Background

In the years immediately prior to Germany's entry into World War II, the Germans conducted many experiments and tests designed to produce satisfactory AA weapons. Even after the experiments conducted during the Spanish Civil War, and the consequent determination to commence extensive manufacture of dual-purpose AA/AT guns, the primary AA purpose of these guns was never lost sight of. The German press gave much publicity to the importance of AA guns in the defense of Germany, and the Government simultaneously proceeded to provide for the activation

---

6 A further treatment of this subject may be found in the discussion of passive means of defense appearing in the following section.

and equipping of AA units in unprecedented numbers. Since plans for employment of these AA units in defense presupposed close cooperation with aviation, the rapidly growing AA forces were made an organic part of the German Air Force. With the outbreak of war, the formation of new AA units for local defense as well as for field service proceeded apace.

18. General Organization of AA Defenses

a. Responsibility

In addition to his other duties, the Chief of the German Air Force is responsible for the defense of territorial Germany and of important installations and cities of the occupied countries. An inspector for each separate arm of the Luftwaffe (similar to our former chiefs of branches) functions directly under the Chief of the Air Force and is responsible directly to the Chief for the state of training and efficiency of the separate elements comprising the rear-area defenses.

b. Defense Districts

For the purpose of home defense as well as for other needs, Germany and the important occupied territories are divided into air territorial areas known as *Luftgaue*. In 1939, 15 of these air territorial districts lay within the borders of Germany. In addition, there were two separate air territories established for areas especially open to hostile air attacks. These comprised the Air Defense Zone, West, which was almost identical with the area covered by the West Wall fortifications, and the Air Defense Zone, Sea, which covered in general the North Sea coastal and island area. Following the French Campaign, the first zone was eliminated. Other *Luftgaue* were organized within the occupied countries, however, to tie in with the general scheme of defense against air attacks.

The commander of a *Luftgau* is subordinate to the Chief of Air Forces alone. Even though his *Luftgau* may correspond in extent and nomenclature to a geographical army corps area, he is in no way subordinate to the army corps area commander. The *Luftgau* commander may have been originally an air officer or an AA artillery officer, or even an air signal officer. There is no rule on the matter other than that he must be an Air Force officer.

Luftgaue coordinate their defenses with each other, in accordance with regulations published by the Chief of the Air Force. The commander of the individual *Luftgau* has specialists who act respectively as commanders of the interception, pursuit, and other aviation; commanders of all AA artillery of the district, including searchlights; and commanders of the signal service employing warning and communication facilities. Other specialists, functioning directly under the district commander, include the commanders of barrage balloon units and of units responsible for carrying out so-called passive-defense measures. The operating units function under the specialist commanders both on direct orders from these commanders, and, when occasion demands, upon the initiative of the unit commander. In actual operations, in most cases the commands above the actual operating units act mainly in a coordinating capacity, feeding information to the operating units who act in turn on their own initiative in accordance with prescribed standing operating procedure.

Within certain of the air districts there are special air defense commands. These cover regions of vital importance whose defense must be insured with a maximum of defense facilities. In these defense commands, of which the cities of Berlin and Hamburg, and the Ruhr district, are typical examples, there are concentrated under a single command sufficient defense facilities of all kinds to prevent the attacking hostile air forces from carrying out their mission.

c. Component Arms

The AA guns are considered the backbone of the static defense, but the operation of the system calls for close cooperation with friendly aircraft, especially fighter planes. Searchlight units as a part of Flak proper play a very important part in the German scheme of air defense, and in certain areas barrage balloons are used quite extensively. The Aircraft Warning Service is a part of the Air Force, and as such has the mission of providing adequate warning of hostile aircraft. Certain passive measures form a very important part of the defense system as a whole; these measures must be considered a definite though intangible weapon, so closely tied in with the entire defense system that they must be considered in this discussion.

19. The AA Command in an Air District
a. Groups and Sub-Groups
The Flak, or AA, command in an air district is divided into "Groups" known as *Flakgruppen*. The Groups in turn are divided into "Sub-Groups" called *Flakuntergruppen*. These types are ordinarily territorial divisions. For example, one of the large industrial cities of Germany is divided into two Groups known as the North and South Groups, and each of these in turn has two Sub-Groups. In addition, there is a Sub-Group for outlying territory east of this town, and one for the northwest approaches.

b. Control Centers
The control center of the Flak defenses is the Group. The Group operates downward through sector controls, which in most cases are the Sub-Groups. These sector controls are the operational headquarters for various purposes—such as, for example, for fire control involving the ordering of barrage fire. The sector control is also used as a communication center. Close liaison is maintained between the Flak organizations and the warning service, and between Flak and air fighter-interception units.

c. Operational Units
Operational units are the battalions, regiments, and higher units. Organization of the individual units above the battalion is not uniform, the exact composition of the unit depending upon the part which it is expected to play in the defense scheme. Thus regiments may be found which consist entirely of searchlight units,

Figure 16.—German 88-mm gun in static position. (Note protection provided for gun crew.)

entirely of gun units, or even of two mixed gun battalions and one searchlight battalion (the pre-war standard). Even batteries may vary in organization, as in the case of gun batteries where the fire unit is composed of six instead of four guns. Although the battalion (*Abteilung*) is considered the basic unit, the necessity of deploying batteries makes it impossible in most cases for the battalion commander to exercise detailed control, and the heavy gun battery is normally the fire unit.

20. Employment of AA Guns

   a. **Static Guns (fig. 16)**

Guns emplaced on permanent mounts or in static positions are generally used throughout the air defense system. The emplacements are usually well prepared, with living quarters for the crews. Calibers of these static guns range from the light 20-mm to the heavy 150-mm guns, most of the latter being permanently emplaced in readiness for both AA and coast defense roles. It is known that the light- and medium-caliber guns are also mounted on the tops of high building's and factories.

b. Use of Towers

Guns engaged in a static role are also emplaced in towers of various kinds. For example, in Berlin there are at least two concrete towers 250 feet square and over 100 feet high. Each of these has a "satellite" tower, a smaller rectangular structure about 350 yards distant. The larger towers each have four heavy AA guns, one being mounted on each corner; the smaller towers each have four light AA guns and what appears to be a radio-location instrument. It is believed that these towers are also used in the control system.

c. Use of Mobile Guns

Mobile guns include those on railway mounts. In some areas a proportion of the gun defenses are mobile so that guns and gun positions may be altered on short notice. In order to achieve the maximum effect, the Germans believe that the system of AA defense should be extremely flexible, and the active means of defense are therefore closely coordinated with the means for deception. Under this system, different positions can be taken by mobile units at different times. For example, if system "A" is used tonight, the mobile force will take position in area 1; if system "B" is selected, they will be installed in area 2, etc. These systems of antiaircraft defense are changed frequently in order to meet changes in the tactics of enemy aviation. The net result theoretically operates to produce confusion in the mind of any hostile aviator who might attempt to orient himself through locations of a series of gun positions based on past experience. Guns emplaced in these positions are nearly always countersunk to permit continuous firing throughout an air raid with maximum protection to the crews.

d. Use of Dummy Guns and Dummy Positions

In keeping with the practices of active deception mentioned in the previous paragraph, the Germans employ dummy gun positions and dummy guns. The latter are usually employed along probable lines of air approach, and it is known that dummy gun flashes have been used. Furthermore, mobile guns may rotate through the various dummy positions, thus precluding any safe conclusions, based on hostile air reconnaissance, as to the existence of a set system of dummy positions.

e. Disposition of AA Guns in Rear Areas

(1) *General.*—In heavily defended areas, heavy guns are disposed on the outskirts with special attention to the expected lines of approach. A certain number of positions will be in the area itself, and will be situated about 6,000 yards apart where the target is a large one. Light guns are concentrated at particularly vulnerable points, such as factories and docks. They are occasionally emplaced on lines of approach, such as canals, rivers, or arterial roads. For isolated vulnerable points, the disposition of defenses is a special problem which varies with the nature of the particular target. For example, airdromes generally have 12 or more heavy guns, none placed nearer than 2 miles, and 12 to 30 light guns, none located nearer to the perimeter than 500 yards.

(2) *Heavy guns.*—(a) *Four-gun positions* (fig. 17).—In the normal four-gun layout, the guns are sited roughly in a square of approximately 70 yards to a side. A fully equipped position has two command posts, which for convenience may be termed Command Post No. 1 and Command Post No. 2. Command Post No. 1 is usually situated about 100 yards to the side of the gun layout, and contains the *Kommandogerät*, which transmits data by cable to a junction box located in the center of the square, and thence to each of the four guns. Command Post No. 2 is located approximately in the center of the square, and normally contains the auxiliary predictor (director), with its separate height- and range-finder. Communication from the auxiliary predictor to each gun is by telephone. The fire is normally controlled from Command Post No. 1; in the event of destruction or failure of the *Kommandogerät* or the transmission system, fire is controlled from Command Post No. 2.

Depending on the terrain, 20-mm guns are normally located

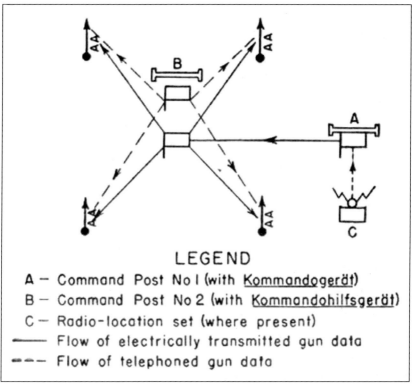

Figure 17.—4-gun layout.

between the gun layout and Command Post No. 1 in order to provide protection against low-flying aircraft.

In a great many cases, the normal four-gun layout has only one command post, either in the center or, more frequently, to the side. The provision of two command posts depends partly on the importance of the locality and partly on the availability of equipment.

It is interesting to observe that wherever the existence of radio-location fire control has been suspected or observed, the equipment has been found on sites with one command post to the side, and always in close proximity to the command post. Where this equipment is used, it is suspected that one set may furnish data for several nearby gun batteries.

(b) *Six-gun positions.*—Six-gun layouts fall into three main categories:—

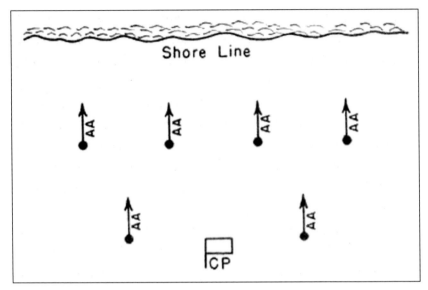

Figure 18. 6-gun layout for coastal defense.

(1) Those expanded from existing four-gun layouts by the addition of two emplacements, one on either side of the original square.

(2) New layouts, consisting either of five guns sites roughly in the form of a circle, with the sixth gun in the center, or of all six guns in the form or a circle.

(3) Coastal layouts, consisting of four guns in a straight line facing the sea, with the remaining two guns in rear (fig. 18). The command post on six-gun positions is almost invariably located outside the gun layout, except in the case of the coastal layouts, where it is usually located between the two landward emplacements.

(3) *Light and medium guns.*—A triangular layout of light and medium guns is common, but not invariable, with the guns anywhere from 75 to 150 yards apart. Guns are seldom deployed singly. In built-up areas, considerable use is made of light guns on specially constructed towers; they are also mounted on the roofs of buildings.

f. Fire-Control Methods

(1) *With heavy guns.*—The Germans use several types of fire-

control methods with heavy AA guns. As has already been indicated, the data-computing director used by the Germans does not differ materially from that used by the U.S. Army, except for the fact that in the latest standard type of director the Germans incorporate the height- and range-finder and the predicting mechanism into one instrument. Since there are times when the target is not seen, or when for various reasons it may not be practicable to rely on fire directed at only one aerial target, the Germans use several methods of fire control, principally the following:

(a) *With director where target is seen.*—This is the normal method and is employed under suitable conditions by day, or in conjunction with searchlights by night. The use of mechanical fuze-setters permits the maintenance of a high rate of fire. Guns may fire singly, but in recent months a tendency towards salvo firing has been observed. At night, targets in searchlight "cones" are engaged by large gun densities, indicating a preference for this type of fire.

(b) *With director where target is unseen.*—This method may be used by day in overcast conditions, or by night in the absence of searchlight illumination. The use of this method presupposes some means, other than visual, of obtaining the basic elements of present azimuth, present angular height, and present slant range. The Germans are known to have experimented with and used searchlight sound locators for this purpose, fixing the location of the target in space by finding the intersection point of data received from two or more separate sound locators. Authentic reports indicate, however, that the Germans have not found the use of searchlight sound locators to be very satisfactory for this purpose. Since the Germans are known to have been employing radio-location instruments since 1940, it is quite certain that such instruments are now being used for obtaining the initial data.

(c) *Predicted concentrations.*—In this method a number of

gun positions operate under a central control or "master station"; gun densities may include as many as 32 guns. Predicted salvos from individual positions have also been encountered. Unless irregular evasive action is taken by the hostile aircraft, both types of fire can be fairly accurately produced by taking a mean of plots of the plane's course.

(d) *Fixed barrages.*—This method was particularly used in the early part of the war. Controlled by a central operations room, the fire can be laid in almost any shape; screen, box, cylindrical, or in depth. This type of barrage is usually put up over a vulnerable point or just outside the bomb release line. At the present time it is used mostly at night or under conditions of bad visibility. Furthermore, the development of up-to-date instruments has made its use secondary.

(2) *With light and medium guns.*—(a) *At visible targets.*—By use of the several course and speed sights, AA fire from light and medium guns is opened With reasonable accuracy, and corrections are made by observation of tracers. The light or medium AA guns are highly maneuverable and can engage a target almost immediately as it comes in view and in range. These guns rely for effect on the high rate and volume of fire. For altitudes below 1,500 feet, they are exceedingly accurate. At very low levels, particularly from 0 to 50 feet, accuracy is considerably reduced, owing partly to the limitation of field of view with a consequent restricted time of engagement, and partly to the high angular velocity of the target in relation to the guns. By night the method of engagement of an illuminated target is similar to that used by day, with greater reliance placed on observation of tracer.

(b) *At unseen targets.*—Against unseen targets, light AA fire is nothing more than a deterrent, as the Germans have no instruments for "unseen" firing with light and medium guns. These guns are sometimes sited close to a heavy searchlight, probably for the purpose of obtaining early approximate data, as well as for the protection of the searchlight.

(c) *Fixed or curtain barrages.*—Fixed or curtain barrages are occasionally fired by the weapons by day or by night over small vulnerable points, at targets or along likely lines of approach.

21. Employment of Searchlights

a. General

The Germans use a large number of searchlights in connection with the AA defense of Germany and important installations of occupied countries. The searchlights have not been particularly successful in illuminating high-flying hostile bombardment planes at night for the sole benefit of gun units. The Germans have learned, however, to use their searchlights for other purposes. Searchlight crews are known to have been dipping their light beams to indicate to their fighter planes the direction in which hostile bombers are flying. Searchlights have also been used successfully to produce "dazzle" and "glare" in efforts to blind and confuse hostile pilots, bombardiers, and gunners. There is now no doubt that all these uses are proving a big help to the Germans in protecting their cities and strategic centers.

b. Equipment

As has already been indicated, the main searchlight equipment used by the Germans consists of the 150-cm (heavy) and the 60-cm (light) searchlights. The latter type is primarily for mobile employment with light Flak batteries. In addition to these two main items of equipment, the Germans also have a limited number of 200-cm and a few French 230-cm lights which are used to supplement the main equipment. Except for mass employment, initial data for the heavy searchlights are usually obtained through the use of sound-locators. With the development of radio-location equipment, there may now be a special set for use with searchlights, but no exact data is available on the extent of development in this field. It should be noted that the light searchlights use no sound locators, picking up their targets by definite searching patterns.

c. Location of Searchlights

Searchlights may be laid out in belts or in concentrations on likely lines of approach to important targets, and around or near gun-defended areas. German searchlights are used to aid night-fighter interception, and those at or near gun target areas are also used to cooperate with Flak. In gun-defended areas, searchlights are used to illuminate aircraft for Flak and for dazzle effect. The spacing of searchlights is as follows:

(1) *In belts.*—A belt usually consists of 10 to 15 or 20 to 30 searchlights, 1,000 to 2,000 yards apart along the course of the belt. The remainder of the lights are 5,000 to 6,000 yards apart.

(2) *In concentrations.*—When used in this manner, searchlights are usually spaced 2,000 to 3,000 yards apart in the shape of a triangle, a circle, or two concentric circles.

(3) *In gun-defended areas.*—Normal disposition is an even spacing approximately 3,000 to 4,000 yards apart. In some special areas, there are small groups with searchlights not more than 1,500 yards apart.

d. Searchlight Tactics

(1) *On cloudy nights.*—Unless a hostile airplane breaks through low-hanging clouds, only a limited number of searchlights, in belt or otherwise, go into action. They attempt to follow the course of the aircraft along the base of the clouds in order to indicate its course to fighters or in order to produce an illuminated cloud effect against which the aircraft might be silhouetted for the benefit of fighters or the AA artillery.

(2) *On nights with considerable ground or industrial haze.*— When the searchlight beams are unable to penetrate the haze, searchlights occasionally go into action at a low angle of elevation on to the haze. They thus diffuse and produce over the target area a pool of light through which the crews of attacking aircraft find identification and orientation extremely difficult.

(3) *On clear dark nights.*—When in belts to aid fighter interception, the most usual functions are: to illuminate the target; to permit

a limited degree of searching in "cone" formation; and, by exposing vertically, to produce ahead of the hostile bomber a wall of light against which it may at some time be visible to fighters attacking from the rear, or to compel the hostile bomber, as it runs the gantlet of lights, to fly so close to one of the beams or group of beams that it becomes visible from the ground, thus enabling other lights to engage. In the parts of belts where the lights are more openly spaced, some beams act as pointers for the benefit of night fighters.

In gun-defended areas, some groups of searchlights produce the maximum degree of dazzle, by exposing (almost vertically) and dousing at fairly regular intervals, and even by waving about in the sky.

Other groups of searchlights possessing a "master" light cooperate with Flak. If illumination is obtained, the guns engage; if not, fire is sometimes directed at the point of intersection of the beam over the target area or just outside the bomb-release line, beams being held stationary until a suitable target presents itself.

(4) *On clear moonlight nights.*—This condition greatly reduces the efficiency of the searchlights. In target areas, tactics are adopted similar to those employed on a clear dark night, except that less attention is paid to dazzle. When attempted, this method has not been able to prevent crews from bombing accurately. In belts, tactics are similar to those employed on a clear dark night, except that a larger number of lights are detailed to indicate the course of hostile aircraft.

e. Dazzle and Glare

"Dazzle" is the blinding of persons in a plane caught in the direct light rays of one or more searchlights. "Glare" means obscuring the target from the plane crew by a light beam played between the plane and the target.

The extent of dazzle is dependent on the height of the plane, the number of searchlights concentrated on it, weather conditions, the direction of the light beams, and to some degree on the reactions of persons in the plane.

Dazzle or glare created by AA searchlights greatly lowers the ability of an aviator to adapt his eyes to seeing at night. Either dazzle or glare makes the location of targets difficult and lessens the accuracy of bombing. Also, keeping beams directly on a plane helps defending fighter-craft to approach the plane unobserved and to attack it more effectively.

22. Employment of Barrage Balloons

Although extensive use of barrage balloons was not planned by the Germans prior to commencement of World War II, very early in the war they made their appearance in certain industrial and strategic towns in western Germany.

The number of balloons in use varies with the considered needs of the area to be defended. For example, they are used in such large numbers over one of the important industrial regions of Germany that a recent observer reported that they were so thick that he "could see several hundred of them at one glance." Although the statement is undoubtedly far-fetched, it well illustrates the psychological value, aside from the practical value, that balloon barrages have.

According to reports, the German balloon barrage usually forms an irregular belt about five-eighths of a mile wide and about 1 3/4 miles from the outer edge of the target area. There is reputedly anywhere from 200 to 800 yards between the balloons. The balloons are flown at varying heights at different times, the exact height and numbers of balloons flown depending on the time of day, the weather, and the threat of aerial attack.

The purpose of the balloon barrage is to form an irregular pattern of perpendicular steel cables in the vicinity of the defended area, presenting a real as well as a mental hazard to any hostile aviator attempting to fly below the level of the balloons. The net result is to discourage hostile flyers from entering the region of the barrage for dive-bombing tactics against the defended area, and to force the hostile planes to an altitude less favorable for precision bombing. The plan for a barrage is coordinated with light-, medium-, and heavy-caliber gun defense, any gaps in the barrage being covered by light and medium Flak. It should also be noted that in defended areas which include harbors and docks, the balloon barrage may extend out over the water, balloons being suspended from stationary or movable barges.

23. Aircraft-Warning System

a. Responsibility

The aircraft-warning service for Germany and for the important occupied areas is the responsibility of the German Air Force, and is a definite integral part of the organization of defense against hostile aircraft. Although a part of the Air Signal Service, for all practical purposes the aircraft-warning service is a separate organization created for the sole purpose of constant observation of the air space over Germany, and for the prompt recognition and reporting of airplanes flying over Germany and other defended zones of the interior. This service is operated through the air district headquarters commanders, to whom the aircraft-warning service is subordinated.

b. Operation

In the operation of this system, there is a fixed "German territorial aircraft-warning service," as well as a mobile aircraft-warning service which is carried out by "aircraft-warning-service companies."

The fixed "aircraft-warning-service net" is mesh-like in character. The distances of individual air guard lines from one another vary between 20 and 45 miles, these distances and lines being established in accordance with tactical considerations. "Air guard stations" comprising observation and reporting stations are generally 6 to 8 miles apart. "Air guard headquarters," comprising plotting and relaying stations, are agencies of the aircraft-warning service. As with our system, the function of the air guard stations is to report the number, type, height, flying direction, identity, etc., of any planes flying over the sector. These reports find their way to a center where they are filtered and evaluated, with subsequent disposition of appropriate information to military authorities as well as to civil protection authorities.

The motorized aircraft-warning companies supplement and increase the density of the fixed aircraft-warning net, as well as being put around a temporarily vulnerable area. Although ordinarily used well forward, they may be employed on open flanks and in rear areas.

The reports of the territorial aircraft-warning service are made by telephone and wire, whereas the reports of the motorized aircraft-warning companies are made by radio.

c. Flak Intelligence Service

The aircraft-warning service is supplemented by the troop-warning service of the German AA artillery, which is similar to the U.S. Antiaircraft Artillery Information Service (AAAIS). Every active German AA unit observes the air in the area under its jurisdiction with specially trained personnel. In addition, all troop units use their own air guards to avoid surprise. The guard gives warning by means of calls, horns, sirens, or blinker lamps.

d. Use of Radio-Detection Devices

It is known that both long- and short-range radio-location instruments are now being used for warning purposes. The long-range instruments are located at intervals along the Western European coast for early warning purposes, and undoubtedly other sets of both long and short range are scattered in a net throughout rear areas to supplement visual observation.

24. Passive Means

In the defense of rear areas, the Germans lay much stress on the use of passive means. These involve every feasible type of deception, including the extensive use of camouflage. No effort has been spared to change the appearance of important potential air objectives as completely as possible. In 3 years of war, the system has been developed to a very high degree of efficiency. AA artillery units cooperate in the system of passive defense by the use of movable defense forces, and through carefully considered gun and searchlight positions. The civil population is well disciplined, and blackout regulations are stringently enforced.

Obviously, it is impossible to conceal the general location of a large military objective such as an industrial city. The Germans recognize this fact, and their attempts to deceive their enemy accordingly include removal of the center of gravity of the defense of the area from the center of the objective area itself. At night this is accomplished largely through the use of searchlights. A hostile flyer will usually fly toward the center of the ring of illumination, since he will assume that the center of the objective should be in that area. Under the German system, the center of the ring of searchlights is accordingly placed to one side of the center of the defended area. Furthermore, the center of the searchlight defense may be moved from time to time, thus precluding any definite "fix" of the center of the searchlight defense with respect to the true objective. For daytime deception, camouflage will be used to a very large extent, no effort being spared to bring about the maximum results.

In line with the German belief that if a considerable portion of the enemy attack can be diverted to dummy objectives, the defense may be considered to have been quite successful, the Germans use complete systems of dummy objectives around their important military establishments. Some of these dummy objectives have been so successful that they have been bombed by hostile aviation many times over. Active means are used to assist the effectiveness of the faked objectives. For example, at night when hostile aircraft bomb the dummy objectives, personnel housed in nearby bomb-proof shelters will start large fires to cause further bombing attempts at the objectives, and to confuse the fliers as to the outcome of their mission. To increase the effect of reality, in many cases the dummy objectives may be protected by AA artillery. Captured materiel is often used for this purpose. Dummy objectives are also placed near the center of the searchlight perimeter. The use of dummy gun positions has already been mentioned. When these positions exist, the mobile section of the active AA artillery defense may move in and out of them. The use of dummy flashes may intermingle with the firing of real AA guns, as a result of which the hostile flier secures a very incorrect picture of the true situation on the ground.

Some examples of the extent of the use of camouflage by the Germans will not be amiss. It is well known that Berlin has been extensively camouflaged, not only the city itself but also the outskirts. One example is that of the most important distinguishing landmark in Berlin, namely, the wide avenue running east and west through the city and called the "Axis." The pavement of this avenue has been sprayed with a dark green paint to blend with the trees in the *Tiergarten* (a large park), along the avenue and throughout the western section of the city. The Victory Monument (*Siegesäule*), in the center of a circle on the Axis, has been painted with a dull color so as not to reflect light. An overhead cover of wire matting, interwoven with green materials to resemble vegetation, covers the avenue for a considerable distance. The wire netting is about 18 feet high and is interspersed with artificial shrubs and trees. About every 30 yards, the coloring and texture of the greenery has been changed. To eliminate shadows, netting has also been hung from the sides at an angle of about 20 degrees.

To create an opposite effect—that is, to simulate a street where in fact there is none—wire netting has also been used. These dummy streets are frequently connected with the real ones, which then disappear into artificial woods. In one instance it is reported that a "woods" was created by fastening artificial sprigs about 1 foot high and about 1 to 2 inches apart to a wire net. Through these "woods" a system of "roads" was painted in brown on the mesh of the net.

Many important buildings in Berlin have been camouflaged

by covering them with nets, and by placing artificial barns, farm buildings, and trees on the roofs. Small lakes have been covered by reed-like mats.

The extent of these camouflage efforts is a good indication of the lengths to which the Germans will go in carrying out large-scale efforts at deception. It may well be expected that no means will be spared to hide the real disposition of gun positions and vital areas.

SECTION V. CONCLUSIONS

25. Conclusions

From an analysis of the contents of this study, certain general conclusions concerning German AA artillery and its employment may be drawn. The most important of these conclusions follow:

1. The organization of German AA artillery units is extremely flexible. The exact composition and size of any AA unit may vary with the specific mission to be performed.
2. Although German AA artillery as an arm is an organic part of the German Air Force, there are some AA units which are organic to higher Army units and are considered as Army troops. These furnish AA protection to the Army units of which they are a part.
3. AA units assigned to an Army field force are subordinated operationally and for command purposes to the Army ground unit with which they are operating.
4. The principal German AA weapons are dual purpose AA and AT weapons which can be and are used in other roles as well.
5. In the approach to battle, and until air superiority has been obtained, German AA weapons which are actually assigned to an AA role remain in that role, except for purposes of self-defense against ground targets or where sudden opportunities for surprise fire against ground targets outweigh the necessity for AA protection. As air superiority is obtained, however, AA

weapons are released for AT missions as well as for other roles against ground targets.

6. At the outset of an operation, depending on the considered need for such use, a certain number of AA guns may be assigned to AT or other artillery roles.

7. The Chief of the German Air Force is responsible for the air defense of Germany and the important areas of occupied countries. This responsibility is carried out through subordinate air territorial districts and special defense commands, all of which contain sufficient fighter aviation, AA artillery with searchlights and barrage balloons, and necessary aircraft-warning-service units to effect a carefully coordinated AA defense.

8. The outstanding feature of the German air defense is the coordination effected by unity of command. All of the means in any single air defense, including fighter aviation, AA artillery, warning services, and civil defense organizations are under one commander, who is alone responsible for the accomplishment of the mission.

ARTILLERY WITH A GERMAN TANK DIVISION

Tactical and Technical Trends, No. 8, Sept. 24, 1942.

The following is a digest of an article written in the Red Star (Moscow) on the use of artillery in a German tank division during attack. It is interesting in that it describes the composition of march columns and attack formations, in addition to discussing tactical employment.

The organic artillery with a German tank division, as used against the Russians on the Eastern Front, normally consists of two 105-mm battalions and one 150-mm howitzer battalion, and is usually reinforced by one or two battalions of light artillery.

On the march, the commanding officers of the artillery regiments, battalions, and batteries, plus a minimum of their respective staffs and control units, march at the head of the column. The artillery reconnaissance party marches with the tank reconnaissance unit. Battery reconnaissance parties consist of two armored cars and two motorcycles. In case one of the cars is destroyed the other can carry on the vital reconnaissance work.

Artillery observers ride in armored cars which are armed with machine guns. In each car there is an observer, the observer's assistant, a radio operator, and a driver. There are two such observation vehicles per battery. The battery commander rides in one and another officer in the other. The battalion has three such observers' cars.

Planes are assigned to work with the artillery of the division and are subject to call by the commanding officer of the artillery who assigns through battalion one plane or more per battery, depending upon the amount of planes available. In the attack, one light artillery battalion normally supports one tank regiment in direct support and the medium battalion is in general support. But in the majority of cases experienced, the artillery of the tank divisions has been reinforced so that two light battalions can be assigned to a regiment in the first echelon, which allows one light battalion per tank battalion. One battery of each battalion supports the right element of a tank battalion, another the left element, while the third is echeloned to the rear and is charged with security of the flanks and rear.

Observation posts, command posts, and battery positions are all moved as far forward as possible. Batteries fire from concealed positions, as a rule.

Preceding an attack, preparation fire is conducted from 15 minutes to 1 hour on enemy artillery and tank assembly areas, and observation points are smoked. Enemy front-line infantry is generally disregarded during the preparation, as their neutralization is left to the tanks. Direct-support battalions do not always participate in the preparation fire, but are put in march order with full supplies of ammunition, ready to jump off with the tanks.

The battalion commanders and battery commanders of direct-support units remain at their observation posts in an attack until the head tank passes their line, at which time they take up their positions in the attack echelons. The German general-support artillery does not change its position in an attack which is designed to go no further than the enemy artillery positions. However, in an attack which is intended to penetrate beyond enemy artillery positions, they do move forward when practicable. If the German infantry lags and is finally held up, but the tanks break through and continue forward, the general-support artillery does not move forward.

During the German break-through at the end of October 1941, from the city of Orel in the direction of Mtsensk, German tank units succeeded in breaking through the Soviet infantry lines, but the German infantry supporting the tanks was cut off and forced to dig in. The support artillery could not move forward and, as a result, the tanks, having no support from their artillery, were compelled, after suffering heavy losses, to return to their original positions.

Comment

The above discussion confirms well-known German tactics. It is important, regardless of the success of the enemy tanks in a breakthrough, to stop the infantry moving up in support of the tanks because the artillery is therefore prevented from advancing and the tanks are deprived of their direct support. The tanks can then be much more easily dealt with.

GERMAN VISUAL SIGNAL SYSTEM FOR ARTILLERY FIRE CONTROL

Tactical and Technical Trends, No. 23, April 22, 1943.

Recently information has come in from German sources of what seems to be a simple visual signal system for artillery fire control in the event of failure of other means of communication. Apparently, it is employed between OP and gun position. Also, it may possibly be used between a forward observer and his communications detachment, when, for one reason or another, it is necessary for the latter to remain at a distance from the observer.

No knowledge of any general signal code is required, and the apparatus can be nailed together and painted in half an hour.

Two disks or panels (see sketches) are required, attached to short rods or handles--such as a barrelhead nailed to a broomstick. The disk is possibly painted half red, half white or whatever other colors that may be more suitable to the background. These disks are used as shown in the accompanying sketches. At night, lights are used.

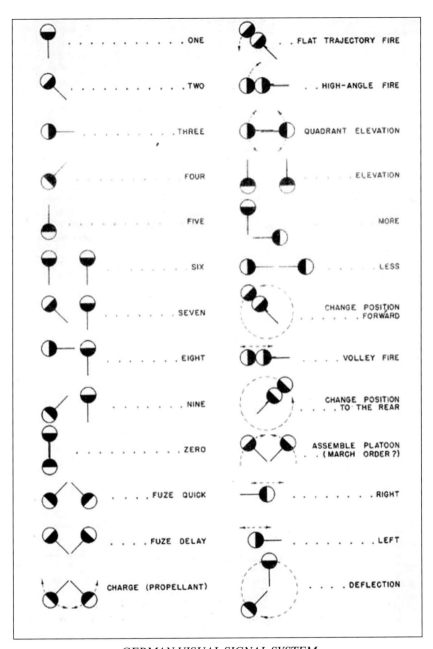

GERMAN VISUAL SIGNAL SYSTEM

75-MM ASSAULT ARTILLERY

Intelligence Bulletin, July 1943.

The German 75-mm assault gun is a weapon comparable to the U. S. 75-mm and 105-mm self-propelled guns. The gun and mount weigh about 20 tons. The maximum speed across country is about 7 miles per hour; on roads, about 22 miles per hour. It can average about 15 miles per hour. On normal roads its radius of action is about 100 miles; across country, about 50 miles. To move an assault-gun battery 100 kilometers (about 65 miles) requires 4,000 liters (about 1,050 gallons) of gasoline. The range of the 75-mm short-barreled tank gun, with which this weapon was originally equipped, is about 6,000 yards.

Apparently there are now three types of German assault guns in service: the short-barreled 75-mm tank gun, with a bore 23.5 calibers in length; the long-barreled 75-mm tank gun, with a bore 43 calibers in length; and an intermediate gun which seems to be a 75-mm gun with a bore 30 calibers in length. It seems probable that the long-barreled 75, which is the principal armament of the new Pz. Kw. 4 tank, may be primarily an antitank weapon, while the intermediate gun will take the place of the old short-barreled 75 as a close-support weapon.

A 1940 German document states that the assault gun "is not to be used for antitank purposes, and will only engage enemy tanks in self-defense or where the anti-tank guns cannot deal with them." However, a 1942 German document states that "the assault gun may be used successfully against armored vehicles and light and medium tanks." This apparent contradiction can perhaps be explained by the fact that prior to the invasion of Russia in 1941, this weapon had been used in limited numbers. Experience in Russia may have shown that it could be used successfully against tanks, although Russian sources refer to it as an infantry support weapon, essentially. Perhaps a more logical explanation lies in two German technical developments since 1940, namely: hollow-charge ammunition, which is designed to achieve good armor-piercing performance at relatively low muzzle velocities, and the reported replacement of the short-barreled, low-velocity 75-mm with the long-barreled, high-velocity 75-mm gun on some of the newer models.

The following information about German assault artillery is a condensation of a recent article in "Red Star," the official Soviet Army publication, and deals with only one of the three types—the short-barreled 75-mm.

The Germans make extensive use of self-propelled guns as assault artillery. Their most important mission is to destroy the opposition's antitank and heavy infantry weapons. The German self-propelled mount under discussion is a Pz. Kw. 3 chassis armed with a short-barreled 75-mm gun, which has a semiautomatic breech block. The gun's traverse is limited. The armor on the front and sides of the vehicle has thicknesses of 50 mm and 30 mm, respectively. The top and rear of the gun carriage is open. The speed of the self-propelled gun is about 31 miles per hour, and its range is about 84 miles. The gun's initial muzzle velocity is about 1,389 feet per second. The gun carries 56 rounds. The ammunition is fixed and consists of the following types: high-explosive, armor-piercing, and smoke.

The gun crew consists of a gun commander, a gunner, a loader, and a driver. Two self-propelled guns make up a platoon. The platoon commander's vehicle is equipped with signal flags, rocket pistols, a two-way radio, and a speaking tube for communication between the commander and his gunner and driver. The radius of the radio is about 2 1/2 miles when the vehicle is at the halt, and from 1 1/4 to a little less than 2 miles when it is moving. The second vehicle in the platoon has only a receiving set and signal flags.

There are three platoons in a battery, as well as a separate gun for the battery commander, three armored vehicles with supplies, and an ordinary supply truck. In a battalion (the largest unit) there is a headquarters, a headquarters battery, and three firing batteries. The battalion commander has a gun under his own personal command. According to the German table of organization, the battalion of assault guns is an independent unit and is part of the GHQ artillery pool. The assault artillery battalion can be placed under the command of an infantry commander or tank unit commander, but not under an officer of lower rank than regimental commander. It is important to note that if an assault-gun battery has the necessary supplies to permit it to take care of itself, it may assume an independent role, apart from that of the battalion.

Assault batteries, which are assigned a limited number of targets, have the mission of supporting the attacks of the infantry, and of destroying the opposition's heavy infantry weapons and strong points disclosed during the course of the attack. In supporting tank attacks, the self-propelled artillery assumes some of the normal tasks of the heavier tanks, including the destruction of antitank guns.

The assault artillery never serves as antitank artillery in an attack; only in self-defense does it open fire at short range, shooting armor-piercing shells against tanks. Its shell has almost no effect against heavy tanks.

The battery is part of the combat echelon, and marches ahead of the trains. All seven guns and three armored supply vehicles are in this echelon. In deploying for battle the guns come first, moving abreast toward the front and ready for instant action. The guns of the platoon commanders are on the flanks. The battery commander is stationed to the rear, in a position which is dictated by the type of firing and the terrain. Behind him, the supply vehicles move by bounds from one protected position to another.

If a position lacks cover, these vehicles follow at a

considerable distance, maintaining radio communication with the rest of the battery.

In carrying out its special task of facilitating an infantry breakthrough into the rear of the opposition's defenses, the assault battery may follow one of two methods of maneuver: the battery may take part in the initial assault, or it may be held in reserve and not committed until the hostile dispositions have been discovered. In all instances the battery cooperates closely with the supported infantry battalion or company.

Assault guns use direct fire. To achieve surprise, they move forward stealthily. In supporting an infantry attack under heavy enemy fire, assault guns halt briefly to fire on target, which offer the greatest danger to the infantry. The assault guns fire a few times, and then disappear to take part in the battle from other positions. When an assault artillery battalion is attached to an infantry division cooperating with Panzer units in an attack, the battalion's primary mission is to destroy the hostile antitank defenses. If the battalion is supporting tanks in a breakthrough, its batteries seek positions permitting good observation. In other cases each battery moves into the attack after the first wave of tanks, and as soon as the latter encounters opposition, the assault guns cover them with protecting fire. It is believed that the Germans regard close cooperation between the assault battery and the first echelon of tanks as essential in effecting a quick destruction of antitank defenses.

If hostile tanks counterattack, the German antitank guns engage them, and the assault artillery unit seeks to destroy the hostile guns which are supporting the attacking tanks. When the German antitank artillery is unable to stop the hostile tanks, as a last resort, the self-propelled assault guns engage the tanks, opening fire on them with armor-piercing shells at a distance of 650 yards or less.

In the pursuit, the assault guns give the infantry close support to strengthen the latter's fire power.

The most important role of the assault battery in defense appears to be in support of counterattacks. However, in special instances, they have been used as artillery to reinforce the division artillery. When an assault battery is to support a counterattack, it is freed from all other tasks. The battery, knowing the limits within which the counterattack will operate, acts just as it would in supporting an infantry attack. Assault-battery officers and infantry commanders jointly make a careful reconnaissance of the area in which the counterattack is to take place.

The most vulnerable points of a German self-propelled assault gun, according to the Russians, are the moving parts, the rear half of the fighting compartment, the observation apparatus, and the aiming devices.

The Russians contend that their antitank rifles and all their artillery guns, beginning with their 45-mm cannon, are able to fight successfully against the German assault guns. Heavy losses of self-propelled guns, the Russians say, have greatly weakened the German Army's aggressiveness in the attack and tenacity in the defense.

ARTILLERY IN THE DESERT

Military Intelligence Service,
Special Series No. 6, November 1942

In the Libyan Desert, where fighting has been continuous, since 1940, fire power has been a decisive factor, and artillery has played an important role in its development. Guns have halted tanks and infantry; guns of all calibers—motor-drawn, self-propelled, portee, and mounted in tanks—have enabled large advances to be made by both sides. Although the primary purpose here is to describe the employment of the artillery's fire power, the broader picture of desert operations, especially insofar as they relate to German tactics, is included as having an important bearing on the whole subject.

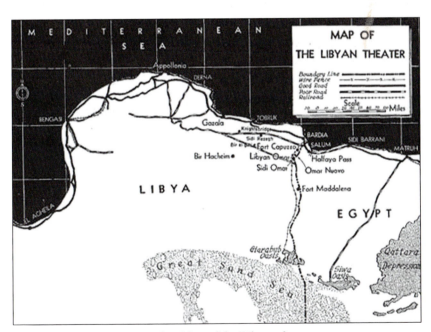

Figure 1.—Map of the Libyan theater

SECTION I. ORGANISATION

General

Both the Axis and the United Nations have been gradually altering their regular organizations to conform to the conditions of the desert. Armored units can carry the fight to the enemy; infantry units, if well balanced, have been able to defend themselves against tank attacks from any direction or against simultaneous attacks from various directions. The traditional infantry-artillery team is able to assume only a defensive role. Independence from the regular supply echelons means greater mobility. Armored units carry more supplies than was contemplated by peacetime training; 7 days' supply is advocated by many officers, and the Germans are said to carry 14. Each unit sent into the desert needs to be as self-sustaining as possible. These are merely some of the factors which must be considered in forming any organization for desert warfare. Well-balanced, closely coordinated teams of armored forces, infantry, field artillery, engineers, antiaircraft, and air forces have been the organizations which have achieved the best results in desert fighting.

German

a. General

It would be an error to attempt to portray any set German organization for tactical purposes. The German varies his organization and the relative strengths of different arms in any force to suit the particular terrain, the nature of the hostile defense, and the missions.

b. Armored Division

The following scheme of organization, subject to many modifications, appears to approximate the normal German armored division as used in the desert:

(1) Headquarters with immediate radio communication to subordinate units and to air reconnaissance and combat support.

(2) Reconnaissance unit.

(a) Armored car company[7] of about 25 armored cars, usually in the proportion of one 8-wheeled car to two 4-wheeled cars.

(b) Support group of motorized infantry including infantry-gun platoon, one antitank platoon, one engineer platoon, and one platoon of heavy machine guns.

(3) One tank regiment of two battalions, each of two Mark III and one Mark IV companies. Each battalion has from 65 to 80 tanks.

(4) One motorized artillery regiment of three battalions, each of three batteries of four guns each; two of these battalions are armed with 105-mm gun-howitzers, and one with 150-mm howitzers.

(5) One motorized infantry brigade, of one motorcycle battalion[8] and of two regiments of two battalions each.

(6) One antitank battalion of three companies of at least 10 guns each. The battalion usually includes some antitank guns on self-propelled mounts.

(7) One light antiaircraft battalion of three companies of twelve 20-mm AA/AT guns each.

(8) One signal battalion; containing a most efficient radio intelligence interception detachment whose interception of enemy messages has been of great value to the German forces.

(9) One engineer battalion, containing a tank engineer company whose task is the support of the tank regiment. This company has two platoons mounted on Mark I tanks, one on armored engineer vehicles, and one on trucks.

(10) Service units. The number and strength of the various services in Libya is not accurately known. The Germans have an excellent tank recovery and maintenance system. Gasoline and ammunition supply vehicles accompany tanks units, and the replenishment system is well organized.

---

7 Some reconnaissance units have two armored car companies.

8 It is believed that Volkswagen have been substituted for the motorcycles, which are unsuited for desert terrain. The Volkswagen as modified for army use is similar to the U.S. "peep." The Volkswagen weighs about 1,400 pounds and develops about 25 horsepower.

c. German 90th Light Division (Afrika Korps)

Throughout the Libyan campaigns the 90th Light Division has operated in the closest conjunction with the 15th and 21st Armored Divisions and has furnished the larger portion of the infantry component of the German "Afrika Korps." In its recently reorganized form, the strength of the division has been estimated at around 12,000 officers and men. The division has a tank battalion and probably between 2,000 and 3,000 motor vehicles.

A large number of auxiliary infantry weapons are included in this division. It would appear, indeed, that the rifle had been relegated to a role of subsidiary importance—a weapon solely for close combat. The backbone of the divisional artillery appears to be the 150-mm assault guns on partially armored self-propelled mounts. The mobility and armor of these weapons permit unusually heavy fire support for the infantry at every stage of battle.

The antitank armament of this division has been strengthened beyond that of any other known German division.

SECTION II. EQUIPMENT

Use Of Enemy Equipment

No attempt is made here to discuss exhaustively the details of all the artillery equipment used in Libya; the more important items are described so that the exposition on tactics which follows can be readily understood.

GERMAN

a. Antitank Weapons

All German forces in the desert have a large number of antitank weapons. Antitank guns have accounted for most of the tanks which the Germans have destroyed. (The details of German antitank guns have been included in Appendix B, which may be consulted for available information on the more important German artillery pieces.)

Figure 2.—German 50-mm antitank gun

b. 50-mm Antitank Gun (fig. 2)

Originally issued to the main units of the German Army in the spring of 1941, this 50-mm. antitank gun is steadily replacing the 37-mm antitank gun, which was formerly the standard German antitank weapon. Both high-explosive and armor-piercing projectiles are fired. The solid projectile fired by this gun weighs 4 pounds 9 ounces, and has pierced the armor of British infantry tanks and cruiser tanks, and of light and medium U.S. tanks. The carriage is provided with an armor-plated shield and has a tubular split trail. This gun is towed on its own wheels and has a detachable third wheel, which attaches to the lunette when the gun crew moves the gun by hand.

- Nature of weapon: high velocity antitank cannon.
- Weight: 2,016 pounds.[9]
- Length of barrel: 62 calibers.
- Traverse: 60°
- Elevation: -13° to +22.5°
- Initial muzzle velocity: 2,953 to 3,280 feet per second (900 to 1,000 meters per second).
- Rate of fire: 16 rounds per minute.
- Weight of armor-piercing shell: 4 pounds 9 ounces.
- Weight of high explosive shell: 3 pounds 15 ounces.

c. 50-mm Tank Gun (high velocity)

This gun is mounted in the new Mark III German tank. It has been very effective at ranges under 800 yards.

- Weight: 421.5 pounds.

---

9 The gun mechanism alone weighs 698 pounds.

Figure 3.—German 28/20-mm antitank gun M41

- Length, over-all: 210 cm (12 feet 11 inches).
- Length of chamber: 30.5 cm (12 inches).
- Length of rifling: 162.2 cm (5 feet 4 inches).
- Muzzle velocity: 3,444 feet per second.
- Weight of armor-piercing shell: 3.9 pounds.
- Rifling: polygroove plane section; uniform twist of 1 in 35 calibers; 16 lands, 3.5 mm wide; grooves, 6 mm wide, .75 mm deep.

d. 28/20-mm Antitank Gun M41 (fig. 3)

The barrel of this semiautomatic gun is constructed on the Guerlich principle; that is, it tapers from 28 mm at the breech to 20 mm at the muzzle. The gun uses the so-called arrowhead type of ammunition. The life of the barrel is thought to be not over 400 rounds. This gun, which has a welded carriage with a split trail, is served by a 5-man crew. It is normally towed portee on a trailer

equipped with ramps and may also be mounted on a truck split into a 5-man load for transport, or carried by air.
- Weight: 501 pounds.
- Muzzle velocity: 4,555 feet per second.
- Caliber at breech: 28 mm.
- Caliber at muzzle: 20 mm.

e. Dual-Purpose Weapons

More and more reports from the desert indicate the use of antiaircraft weapons for antitank purposes wherever such use has become necessary. The Germans have various dual-purpose weapons, the most famous in the desert and elsewhere being the 88-mm.

The German 20-mm AA/AT gun as used in the desert may be towed by a light tractor. There is a four-barrel type, called "Flakvierling" by the Germans.

In addition to the 88-mm, the Germans have two other types of dual-purpose guns which are used extensively. There is the 37-mm AA/AT gun, which is motor-drawn or self-propelled on a half-track vehicle, and the 47-mm AA/AT gun, which originated in Czechoslovakia.

f. 88-mm Dual-Purpose Gun (fig. 4)

(1) Development.—The German 88-mm dual-purpose gun was designed in 1934 as the standard semimobile antiaircraft gun. It is known that the plan of its designers was to construct a dual-

Figure 4.—German 88-mm dual-purpose gun on special trailer

purpose antiaircraft and antitank weapon. It was first used in 1936 during the Spanish Civil War, with considerable effect, on the lightly armored vehicles of the Loyalist forces. The antitank purpose of the weapon was, however, veiled in some secrecy, and the German intentions in this regard did not become well known until the Polish campaign of 1939. The Germans produced large quantities of armor-piercing ammunition and designed a more mobile carriage. With these added improvements the gun was used successfully in the Battle of France, where it proved capable of dealing with the heavier French tanks against which the standard German 37-mm (1.45 inch) antitank gun was comparatively ineffective.

Commencing in 1940, the Germans began to provide these guns with an armored shield in order to protect the personnel against small arms bullets and shell fragments, as well as smaller antitank gun projectiles. The Germans next provided the gun with a new mounting (designated Trailer 201) from which the gun could engage tanks without being taken off its wheels. Finally a self-propelled mounting has been produced from which the gun can be fired against ground targets but cannot be used in its original antiaircraft role.

It appears that this weapon has played an important role throughout the Russian campaign. However, far more exact information is available as to its use in Libya.

(2) Tactics.— In November 1941, when General Auchinleck launched his major offensive, Marshall Rommel formed three tank-proof localities along his front line: at Bardia, at Salum, and in the vicinity of Halfaya Pass. Wherever these areas included 88-mm guns, the guns were used to provide the core of the all-around protection so necessary in the desert against tank attacks. These guns were supported by a large number of smaller antitank weapons. So well organized were these strong points that they were never seriously attacked, and only fell when the British pushed on to Bengasi and when the water and food stocks of the strong

points became exhausted. The British ascribe the long resistance by these strong points to the difficulty they found in coping with these dual-purpose weapons.

Rommel's offensive use of these weapons is of considerable interest. The antiaircraft guns appear to follow closely his armored vehicles. As soon as the front begins to stabilize, the 88-mm dual-purpose guns go into position and around them is then organized a "tank proof" locality.

The effectiveness of these weapons is clearly brought out by the following reports of observers formerly at the front in the desert battle around Tobruk:

One observer reports as follows:

> At a point in the Knightsbridge area, the 4th British armored brigade faced some 35 German tanks of the Mark III and IV type drawn up in line and obviously inviting attack. These tanks were supported by a battalion of 12 antiaircraft guns. The commander of the 4th Brigade refused to attack at all because of the presence of these guns on the battlefield.
>
> Slight firing occurred throughout the day. Towards evening the superior British tank force withdrew, and the German tanks attacked after nightfall in a new direction. Their 88-mm dual-purpose guns had checked the British all day and permitted Rommel to seize the initiative as soon as the British threat had vanished.

Another report reads as follows:

> The greatest single tank destroyer is the German 88-mm dual-purpose gun. For example, on May 27th at 0800, Axis forces having enveloped Bir Hacheimn, a German tank force of 60 tanks attacked the British 22nd Brigade some distance to the northeast. The British moved to attack this force with 50 light and medium American tanks. It soon became apparent that this British force was inadequate and the Brigadier commanding ordered a second regiment of 50 tanks into action. In 10 minutes the 88-mm German dual-purpose guns destroyed 8

American medium tanks of this reinforcing regiment. All day thereafter, the British engaged the enemy half-heartedly and finally withdrew. Sixteen American medium tanks were lost in all. These 16 fell victims, without a single exception, to the 88-mm dual-purpose gun.

(3) Fire-control methods.—For field artillery tasks, and for use against armored vehicles, the following four methods of fire control are used: direct fire using a telescopic sight; predictor control; fire directed from an observation post (OP); and air burst HE.

(a) Direct fire.—This has been the most successful method against armored vehicles. Apart from the extreme mobility of the gun, the efficient telescopic sight has contributed largely to the success of the 88-mm gun in the antitank role.

The latest mark of telescopic sight used is the ZF. 20 E., which is a monocular type with a magnification of 4 and a field of view of 17.5°. The graticule of the sight is formed with two cross lines, interrupted at the center.

On the sight are a range drum graduated in 100-meter (109-yard) steps from 0 to 9,400 meters (10,340 yards), a target elevation drum in 1/16° from 0° to 12°, and vertical and lateral deflection drums. The layer lays on the target through the sight, and the range is set on the range drum, which automatically applies the necessary target elevation to the sight. Corrections from observation of fire or laying off for a moving target are set on the appropriate deflection drums.

(b) Predictor control.—With a predictor control, the data for the first round is calculated in the same way as for an aerial target. Corrections for line, range, and fuze length are made from observation of fire and set on the respective scales on the predictor.

(c) Fire directed from an OP.—When the target is below the horizontal, or at ranges greater than 10,340 yards (that is, beyond the limit of the telescopic sight), fire is directed from

an OP. The OP officer takes bearing, range, and elevation from his shooting map. From these he calculates the gun data with a range table and forwards the information to the gun position by telephone. A director is sometimes used for giving the original line to the guns. Corrections are ordered from observation of fire and set at the gun.

(d) Air burst HE.—Fire for effect with time fuze airburst HE against troops in the open and against battery positions has also been reported. Ranging is carried out with a low height of burst. Fire for effect follows with the fuze length adjusted for the most effective height of burst.

(4) Service of the piece.— The 88-mm unit, which is under divisional control for tactical purposes, goes into action from the ammunition line. Here the ammunition trucks are left, and the battery commander, the chief of section, and the driver reconnoiter the assembly point, usually within 225 yards of the gun position, in march order, and the crew prepares it for action when the command is given at the assembly point.

The gun crew is composed of a gun commander and nine men. The service of the gun for antitank fire is divided among them as follows:

- Gun commander:
- No. 1: Lays for elevation
- No. 2: Lays for line
- No. 3: Loads and fires
- Nos. 4, 5, 6, 7: Handle ammunition
- No. 8: Sets range (vertical deflections)
- No. 9: Sets lateral deflections

(5) Characteristics.—The German 88-mm dual-purpose gun, which was used in such effective fashion in the desert, was designed primarily as an antiaircraft weapon, but like many German antiaircraft guns, it may also be employed against ground targets as explained. The high muzzle velocity and the resultant striking power of this weapon make it particularly effective against

armored targets and fortified gun positions, even at considerable ranges. Using HE and armor-piercing ammunition, it is employed with deadly effect against medium and heavy tanks.

(a) Gun.—The barrel is jacketed, with easily detachable breech rings, a supported, interchangeable A tube (the rifled part of the tube), and a removable guide ring. It is 16 feet long and has 32 rifling grooves. The breech is semiautomatic and self-cocking, opening when the barrel runs out after the shot has been fired, ejecting the cartridge case, and at the same time compressing the striker spring.

(b) Carriage.—The carriage consists of a mounting built into the platform of the chassis, the upper carriage with a protective armor shield, a buffer fitted into the barrel cradle, a hydropneumatic recuperator fitted above the barrel, two balancing springs to distribute the excess weight of the barrel and cradle, and the traversing and elevating mechanism.

(c) Sight.—The standard German antiaircraft sight, modified to give range readings in meters rather than elevation angles, is normally used, but the armor shield also has a loop-hole for the wide-angle (emergency) sight. With the telescopic sight, the line of sights is parallel to the axis of the barrel when both deflection and range drums are set at zero. Since, however, the sight is 28 inches to the right of and 8 inches below the barrel, the aiming point must be taken low and to the right if direct hits are to be obtained.

The elevation field is determined by fixing an attachment on the sextant from -3° to +15°. The traverse field is limited by the striking of the upper carriage against the armor of the driver's seat. The traversing arc is 151° to the right and 181° to the left, or a total traverse of 332°

(d) Mobility.—Two methods are still used to give the gun its well-known mobility: (1) some of the guns are mounted on the special trailer (No. 201) which is fitted with pneumatic tires and drawn by a half-track vehicle which carries the gun

crew and a small supply of ammunition. Ground targets can be engaged while the gun is in this traveling position. (2) the newer development is the self-propelled mounting consisting of a 12-ton half-track vehicle, armored in front and carrying a small supply of ammunition. The gun mounted in this position is used only for engaging ground targets.

Rules on the selection of a firing position are as follows: the angle of impact should be not greater than 60°; the range should generally not exceed 2,000 yards; the gun level must slope downward with the wheels nearer the target lower (the gun level varies from -3° to +15° from the horizontal of the muzzle); the position should be concealed and as near to the target as possible to insure maximum accuracy and surprise in opening fire; the lanes of approach and withdrawal must be as firm and level and as wide as possible.

The prime mover can knock down trees up to 3 inches in diameter, and the self-propelled carriage can level 5-inch trees. The minimum widths, which must be considered in choosing lanes of approach and withdrawal, are: with barrel at right angles, 20 feet; with side supports in rest position, 16 feet; and with side supports in march position, 10 feet. If narrow points have to be negotiated on the way to the firing position, the side supports are not put down until these points are passed, nor is the barrel swung free until there is sufficient room. At all times, however, the barrel, with its armored shield, is directed toward the enemy.

(e) Summary.—Following is a list of characteristics of the German 88-mm dual-purpose gun (on towed carriage):
- Muzzle velocity: 2,690 feet per second
- Maximum ordinate: 36,000 feet
- Maximum horizontal range: 16,200 yards
- Effective range against tanks: 3,000 yards
- Effective ceiling: 34,000 feet
- Elevation: -3° to +85°
- Traverse: 360°
- Weight of piece in firing position including outriggers:

11,354 pounds
- Weight of tube: 3,175 pounds
- Caliber: 88-mm
- Length in calibers: 56
- Height of tube over outriggers: 52 inches
- Height of tube over earth: 63 inches
- Longest recoil: 41 inches
- Shortest recoil: 28 inches
- Weight of trailer: 16,426 pounds
- Tread: 70 inches
- Diameter of wheels: 36 inches
- Weight of projectile: 21 pounds
- Weight of propelling charge: 20 pounds
- Weight of bursting charge: 1.5 pounds
- Rate of fire: 15 to 20 rounds per minute

g. 75-mm Sturmgeschütz (Assault Gun)

The Germans have mounted their 75-mm Kw. K.[10] (used also as the main armament of the Pz. Kw. IV)[11] on the chassis of their Pz. Kw. III. The turret is removed and replaced by a squat superstructure housing the gun. The gun compartment is roofed, but there is no rotating turret. The gun is fitted with a dial, not a telescopic sight. The gun commander has a scissors telescope. Two wireless receivers and one transmitter[12] are carried. There is no mounting for a machine gun. The armor is 55 mm (2.17 inches) at the front, 30 mm (1.18 inches) at the sides, and 12 mm (0.47 inches) on top. Inside this moving pillbox, a crew of four are required: the commander (on the left), the driver, gunner, and leader (on the right).

This gun is employed in independent battalions. It is possible that these assault guns have now become organic parts of the motorized and Panzer divisions, as well as part of the front-line infantry divisions. Normally only direct fire is used. It is believed

---

10 Kraftwagen Kanone, tank gun.

11 Panzer Kraftwagen, armored vehicle, tank.

12 Type B. UA2.

that this low-velocity 75-mm gun is being replaced by a high-velocity 75-mm gun with a reported length of bore of about 43 calibers.

An assault gun of this type captured in the Middle East has been described as follows:

The gun and mount weigh about 20 tons. The gun itself is the short-barreled 75-mm tank gun originally mounted in the Mark IV tank. The range drum is graduated for HE up to 6,550 yards and for AP up to 1,640 yards. Elevation and traverse are hand-operated. The hull is that of the standard German Mark III tank with normal suspension system. The turret has been removed. The length is 17 feet 9 inches, height 6 feet 5 inches, and width 9 feet 7 inches. In general, the armor is 51 mm (2 inches) at the front and 32 mm (1.25 inches) on the sides and at the rear. An added 53-mm plate is fitted to the rear of the vertical plate, apparently between the driving and fighting compartments, and is braced to the front plate by two 31-mm plates, one on each side of the opening for the gun. The sides of the hull enclosing the driving compartment appear to be vulnerable to the British 40-mm antitank ranges. The engine is a Mayback V-12-type rated at 300 horsepower. The gears provide for six speeds, and steering is hydraulically controlled. The capacity of the gasoline tank is 71 gallons, which is consumed at the rate of about 0.9 miles per gallon at a cruising speed of 22 miles per hour. As in German tanks, this vehicle is equipped to carry extra gasoline in a rack on the rear of the vehicle, which should hold about 10 standard 5-gallon gasoline cans. The captured vehicle contained metal boxes for 44 rounds of ammunition, and 40 rounds were stacked on the floor at the loader's station. Ammunition is also carried in an armored half-track vehicle which tows an armored ammunition trailer. There was also a rack for 12 stick grenades, and the usual smoke-candle release mechanism for 5 candles was fitted to the rear. For communication there were two radio receivers and one transmitter. For observation a scissors telescope was provided. As spare parts the 11-mm sloping plates over the track guard carried two spare bogie wheels on the right side and one on the left side. Two spare torsion rods were also carried, one in each side of the hull above the bogies. Some other details are—

- Length of bore: 23.5 calibers.
- Muzzle velocity (estimated): 1,600 feet per second.
- Elevation: 20°.
- Depression: 5°.
- Traverse: 20°.
- Weight of projectiles: HE, 12 pounds 9 ounces; Smoke, 13 pounds 9 ounces; AP (with ballistic cap), 13 pounds 9 ounces; AP (hollow charge), not known.
- Estimated penetration of AP: 55-mm (2.16 inches) with ballistic cap at 60° at 400 yards.

h. Russian 76.2-mm Gun

It is reliably reported that the Russian 76.2-mm field gun is being used in Libya by the Germans for antitank purposes. Published photographs of this weapon indicate that it is a practical high velocity weapon.

Use Of Enemy Equipment

a. General

In the fast moving situation in the desert, where the tide of battle changes quickly, considerable effort has been made to use captured enemy materiel in boomerang fashion. There have been many instances of captured enemy guns being manned by their captors.

The four-gun 75-mm battery captured in Omar Nuovo was manned by the regimental headquarters personnel of one regiment and the lost infantrymen of another division. They fired over a 1,000 rounds back at the Italians and took part in the bombardment of Libyan Omar.

Extensive use was made of captured machine guns, antiaircraft weapons, artillery, tanks, and motor vehicles captured from time to time throughout the operations in Syria. Considerable use was made of captured weapons in the British defense of Tobruk.

b. Use of Captured Italian Weapons

The British have captured large amounts of enemy matériel, particularly Italian. The use of all these captured field artillery weapons has been limited by a lack of spare parts, the recoil systems, both spring and hydro-pneumatic, having suffered particularly. The carriages of the 100-mm and 149-mm howitzers are old models, and the best performance from these weapons can be expected only when they are mounted on modern carriages. None of these weapons is considered suitable for mobile operations in the desert, but they are satisfactory under static conditions. Although some of the Italian weapons have not proved satisfactory enough to be used by the British, some have been used with interchangeable British ammunition and parts and others with Italian ammunition.

Ammunition

A direct hit at close ranges from a 105-mm gun or a 25-pounder has usually knocked out the tank or the crew, regardless of the point of impact. High-explosive shells are always useful against personnel in the open and in light shelters. Flashless powder is highly desirable, especially for medium and heavy artillery, which are the favorite targets of dive bombers, strafing fire, and enemy batteries. Weapons have been difficult to detect at a distance when using this type of propellant. The use of separate-loading ammunition places any weapon at a disadvantage during action against armored vehicles.

The Germans give much attention to the effect of the tropical sun on their munitions and weapons. All ammunition other than small arms ammunition is especially packed for the Tropics. All munition cases are so marked. Normal charges for tropical use are calculated at an average temperature of 77° Fahrenheit.

Caissons have been found to be one of the best means of stowing ammunition, because they both protect the ammunition and make it readily available and mobile.

Protection is needed because of the vulnerability of shells and fuzes piled on the ground. The explosion of stacked ammunition set afire by an aircraft cannon wiped out in one instance two Bofors crews. It is true that stacked ammunition can be dug in for protection against shell fire and air attack. However, the mobile operations of the desert give little time for digging protective pits for ammunition—in fact, there is hardly ever sufficient time to dig slit trenches for personnel. Protection at the guns cannot be given by trucks, because they are too conspicuous and vulnerable to be allowed to remain at gun positions as ammunition carriers. Dumped ammunition can seldom if ever be saved in the sudden moves of armored action. Caissons are the British solution to all these difficulties.

The British use artillery trailers between the 25-pounder gun and its prime mover. Two trailers are also coupled behind a prime mover to form the ammunition section. Each trailer can carry 32 rounds of 25-pounder ammunition and fuzes, plus some extra space for a small amount of supplies. These loaded trailers are dropped near the gun positions and give some protection against air attack and shelling, serving the same purpose as horse artillery caissons.

SECTION III. TACTICS

Introduction

This section on the tactical employment of artillery in the North African campaigns is influenced by two considerations:

a. The Task-Force Principle.

The development of the task-force principle underlines the importance of the coordinated tactical action of all arms. Therefore, while the main focus here is on artillery action, this will always be referred to the general operations in which artillery plays its part.

b. Special Conditions of Desert Warfare.

The terrain and climate of this theater have imposed certain limitations and set certain problems, some of which involve or affect the use of artillery.

Reconnaissance

a. General

Both large and small units operate over wide desert expanses. The lack of cover necessitates great dispersion, which in turn requires each unit to provide its own close-in defense—a situation emphasizing the need of reconnaissance.

Constant use is made of both ground and air reconnaissance units. Even the side which is weaker in air strength carries on air reconnaissance. Forward ground reconnaissance is usually executed by armored cars. Frequently German armored car patrols are supported by tanks, in a ratio of one tank to two armored cars, to provide sufficient fire power to overcome hostile patrols and outposts and thus extend the depth of observation. Once contact is gained by the Germans with an armored force, it is kept under observation even though the German armored units may have withdrawn. As a result, German armored units have been able to avoid battle when conditions were not favorable, to make night attacks against bivouacs, and even to surround hostile bivouacs during the night with antitank weapons and destroy the armored vehicles from close range in the morning.

b. Methods of Observation

Although the desert is not completely flat, suitable vantage points for observation posts are never very high. This lack of height, together with the heat waves rising from the hot sand and rocks, sometimes reduces visibility in the desert. Mid-day is the least satisfactory period for observing fire.

Both sides endeavor to gain what high ground does exist in the desert. It has been noted that the German infantry in Libya, as elsewhere, have launched attacks for the purpose of obtaining observation posts for their artillery. In one instance such an attack was made to gain ground only 3 feet higher than the surrounding terrain.[13] Similarly, German artillery officers have been known to

---

13 This conforms with modern German tactical doctrine. In "Tactical Handbook for the Troop Commander" by General Friedrich von Cochenhausen, the general doctrine on artillery and infantry cooperation is stated: "The infantry must seize and hold the terrain most suitable for artillery

ride on top of tanks in order to gain height for observation.

In both German and British armored divisions the artillery has its own armored vehicles for observation posts. However, even artillery with unarmored troops utilizes methods similar to those of the armored divisions. Forward observers are well out in front with those covering forces, armored cars, or carriers which are deployed for reconnaissance and outpost duty. Often these mobile OP's must be with the armored-car screen, and they are then in an armored car or scout car. Many British officers have spoken highly of the U.S. M-3 Scout Car for this work. Its chief advantage is that it accommodates the entire OP party, whereas the armored car has room for only three persons. Armored cars or scout cars are assigned to and maintained by artillery units. Enough cars must be provided so that all radio sets allotted to a battalion can be mounted in such vehicles; these can then be used by forward observers. The advisability of providing more than a few such cars has been quickly realized, because they wear out soon and have a high casualty rate. Unless the OP is the same type of vehicle as that used by the supported troops, the enemy will concentrate its fire power on the OP vehicle.

The British have found it to be impossible to assign tanks to artillery for OP purposes. But they do have arrangements whereby each regiment of tanks modifies and, on occasion, reserves for artillery observers a certain number of tanks.

A problem of observation was revealed in one fast-moving situation which occurred during the winter of 1941-1942. The battery commander was traveling with the tank regimental commander. Two observers, one per troop,[14] were directing fire while traveling with the forward elements of the regiment. When contact was actually made, the observers had their tanks stay on the flanks and drop back slightly from the front in order to avoid becoming directly engaged. All control was by radio and the

---

observation posts. The movable artillery observation posts accompanying foremost infantry units are the only guarantee for intimate cooperation."

14 British troop is equivalent to U.S. battery.

observer had his own radio operating in the artillery net, separate from the tank radio which operated in the tank net. Because of the limited number of frequencies available, it was necessary for all artillery units in a battery to be on the same frequency. The effect of this single frequency was unfortunate, for only one troop could be fired by one observer at a time, and a great deal of confusion occurred. When all control by observers breaks down, artillery support deteriorates into direct laying by individual pieces.

In addition to the armored OP's, gun towers have been used to gain height for observing fire. These OP ladders are used both as dummies to draw fire and for observation. They are mounted on trucks or may be removed quickly and set up at an OP. The British observing towers are generally about 25 feet high. The Germans have a two-piece telescoping tube mounted on the side of their armored OP, which can be cranked up into observing position. To employ these gun towers effectively there must be a number of them—at least one to each four guns. These, like the tanks and the slight rises in the ground, aid in overcoming the flatness of the desert.

Other difficulties arise in the desert which only keen eyes and training can surmount. There is the real problem which a forward artillery observer has in identifying his own bursts among the dust and heat waves when other units are also firing. Judging distance in the desert is as difficult as on the ocean. Lack of familiarity with the size and appearance of armored vehicles at various ranges is a frequent cause for misjudging distance. The fact that the enemy opens fire does not inevitably mean that the enemy is within range, for he can misjudge distance also. But it is even more important to remember that all tanks are not equipped with the same type of gun. German tanks armed with 75-mm guns can open effective firing at a range of 2,000 yards. Antitank guns with a smaller range waste ammunition by returning fire and, what is worse, give away their own positions.

Selection And Occupation Of Positions

a. Introduction

Suitability of position for accomplishing the mission assigned, and also cover and camouflage, are sought by the artillerymen in the desert as elsewhere. Since cover is practically impossible to obtain in most desert positions, the main concern in selecting a gun position is the suitability of the soil for digging pits and the possibility of arranging for mutual support with other units.

b. Terrain

Both sides make excellent use of those few accidents of the ground which occur in desert terrain. Maximum use is made of folds of the ground both to advance and to conceal tanks, artillery, and antitank weapons. Artillery and antitank guns have frequently been cleverly concealed in ground where the terrain was unfavorable for tank action.

Quick concealment from both the ground and air is obtained by digging gun pits and using light-colored camouflage nets. Gun pits which have no parapet, being flush with the surface of the ground, are more easily concealed than those which have. When possible, therefore, both Axis and United Nations troops distribute the soil and refrain from building a parapet. Gun pits are dug to permit all-around fire.

Often a diamond formation with sides of about 800 yards is employed for a regiment of four batteries. This enables the batteries to be mutually supporting. The guns within each battery are sited in semicircular fashion, 60 to 70 yards apart.

On going into action, the British consider the priority of tasks to be:

(a) Concealment from ground and air;

(b) Digging of slit trenches;

(c) Digging of gun pits, command posts, etc.

Rapidly occupied positions may not be the best available. Therefore, reconnaissance for more satisfactory gun positions is always carried out in such circumstances, and a move is made as soon as possible. In the event of a severe shelling, batteries move to alternate positions if the new positions will still give the necessary mutual support.

c. Dispersion

Both dive-bombing and strafing aviation seek out artillery units for attack, as they are profitable targets. To defend against such attacks, either cover or dispersion is necessary. Since sufficient cover is not usually available, the dispersion of vehicles has been great—200 yards between vehicles being normal. Units spread out in this fashion offer no target for air attacks. When the enemy air force has been inactive, the distance between vehicles is sometimes reduced. This is done to insure better defense against tank attacks and to obtain more control over units. A New Zealand division, while in defense of the Sidi Rezegh-Belhamed area, reduced the distance between its vehicles because of the small amount of cover available, and vehicles at 50- to 60-yard intervals did not suffer undue casualties during artillery bombardments. Undoubtedly casualties would have been severe if there had been an enemy air attack on that occasion.

d. Camouflage

In the desert every gun is dug into a pit if time permits, and covered with a net; every tent is set in a pit and camouflaged; and even each tank has a canvas top placed over it to make it look like a truck. All vehicles are painted with nonglare sand-color paint, and all glass is smeared with oil or a glycerine solution, and then dirt is thrown on these surfaces. Only a narrow unsmeared slit on the windshield is left to obtain vision. Wheel tracks are everywhere and cannot be disguised or obliterated.

A liberal application of dull yellow paint—the color of the sand—has been found to be the best method of rendering both artillery pieces and motor trucks less visible in the desert. The outlines of a piece are broken by the use of scrub and sand mats. The barrel and cradle are sometimes painted a dull sandy color, except for a 1-foot diagonal stripe of light brown or green to break up the pattern of the gun. Motor vehicles carry camouflage nets, which are stretched taut from a central position on the roof of the vehicle at an angle of not more than 45°, and then pegged to the ground and covered with threaded screen and bleached canvas, or with pieces of sandbags 50 to 70 percent of which are painted dull yellowish white. The vehicles themselves are painted cream white, broken by irregular patches of light brown or green. The object is to neutralize dark shadows by an equivalent amount of dull white. Germans and British have adopted this sand color as camouflage. During recent operations German tanks were painted black, evidently to aid their antitank gunners in quick daytime identifications while also serving as night camouflage.

As a security measure and to prevent unauthorized persons gaining information regarding the identification of units and movement of troops, by observing motor transport movements, the practice of marking vehicles with unit designations has been discontinued. A code system, employing color and combinations of colors with numbers to indicate various tactical organizations has been adopted.

Communication

a. General

Distance is the principal problem encountered in desert communications. Radio is used extensively, as wire is laid only when there is time—an element often lacking in desert operations. Radio presents a unique problem of security, because radio communication is like shouting from place to place—all who will can listen. This has necessitated the development of various codes and devices for the secret transmission of data by radio.

b. Visual Signals

Although visual signals are not used extensively for transmitting artillery data, flag signals are employed by both sides for short messages and for identification, especially in small tank units. Recently, the Germans had radio sets in a ratio of one set to three tanks. The three operated as a unit, flag signals being used to control the tanks which had no radio. Great use has also been made of pyrotechnic signals. Recently, two signals were used by the Germans to identify their tanks to German aircraft: a Very signal of three white stars, and an orange-colored smoke. Large flags have sometimes been used for the same purpose. Rockets have been used in profusion at night, apparently both to rally forces which were scattered when dark fell, and to confuse and harass the enemy. It is not known what method the Germans use to identify tanks to friendly antitank and artillery weapons. When the British used the method of approaching friendly troops with turret guns pointing to the rear, the Germans were quick to adopt the same method for purposes of deception, in order to approach close to hostile weapons.

c. Wire

Although the speed of operations in the desert may on occasion preclude the use of telephone lines, a greater degree of security and dependability is achieved by using wire. Almost all lines are laid on the ground. Motor vehicles traveling across the desert constantly are running over the wires. The results of bruising of wire are not so serious in the desert, since ordinary field wire operates better over the desert surface than it would over damp or moist ground. Also, laying and picking up wire are much less difficult in the desert than in swampy or wooded country. Of course, overhead wire circuits are more desirable when the situation becomes at all static. Communication over long field lines in most cases is good in the desert.

The wide dispersion of guns has made necessary the use of an enunciator system between the executive and the individual sections of the firing batteries. Such a system permits the executive to coordinate and command his guns in such a manner as to control rapidly the guns for effective concentrated fire.

d. Radio

Radio is the most important means of communication in the

desert. During the summer of 1941 one British armored division conducted its entire communication network by radio. Every command vehicle had a receiving set. Each artillery troop has three No. 11 sets using one principal frequency, and, for emergency use, one switch in "frequency."

Each troop of this armored division was part of a mobile column, which furnished No. 9 command sets. Switch frequencies were in the overlap band of No. 10 and No. 11 sets, permitting use of No. 9 in displacement by a half-troop in case no extra infantry No. 11 set was available for the purpose. Artillery troops normally operated with two OP's using No. 11 sets. A third OP could be manned for emergency use by diverting a set from the infantry of the mobile columns.

Only one radio set could be provided to each gun position. This may have been caused by the fact that British radio sets are heavy and cannot be removed from the vehicle in which they are mounted. The range of the No. 11 set—voice, 15 miles—has been considered adequate for all troops used during the summer of 1941.

e. Codes

During active operations all messages below the division are usually sent in the clear. Christian names of tank and unit commanders and prearranged code names for places are used. Although there is little intentional enemy interference with artillery communications, there are active and efficient Axis radio-interception intelligence units.

The use of plain language even when accompanied by code names and enciphered place names enables radio interception to be employed effectively. By keeping a careful record of all names, key words, and numbers, both the Italians and the Germans have been able to bring their order-of-battle information up to date by a process of sifting and cross indexing. Officers' names, either family name or given name, are the principle keys used in identifying intercepted messages. Captured German documents indicate

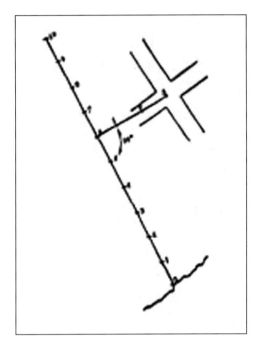

Figure 15.—The "thrust line"

that the careful compilation of names made by the Germans has enabled them to work out British code names. In addition to names, references to the personnel arm, such as "Gunner Smith," or "Rifleman Jones," have helped the Axis forces to identify said units.

One of the most interesting methods of enabling map references to be sent in the clear with security is the "thrust line" method used by the Germans. (This method is similar to the code described in FM 18-5, "Organization and Tactics of Tank Destroyer Units," June 16, 1942, paragraph 231 b (2) (e).) It consists of a line drawn upon a map which theoretically may run in any direction but which actually usually extends in the proposed direction of advance or down the axis of a reconnaissance unit.

The line, which begins at a fixed point and continues indefinitely in the required direction, is usually divided into centimeters for convenience. To give a map reference, a perpendicular is dropped from the reference point to the thrust line. Measurements are then taken from the point of origin to the point where the perpendicular cuts the thrust line, then along the perpendicular to the reference point. Since the point may lie on either side of the thrust line, the second figure must be prefaced by either "right" or "left", as one looks toward the enemy.

A typical reference would be "6 right 3." (See fig. 15.) The figures are always in centimeters; therefore, the actual distance on the ground will vary with the scale of the map used. The scale may start with an arbitrary figure, and have dummy figures interspersed, or it may start with the number of the thrust line when there are several in a given area. These devices make the code difficult to break rapidly.

Instruments have been found consisting of a transparent ruler graduated in millimeters, with a shorter ruler similarly graduated and fixed to slide up and down at right angles to the longer ruler. Practiced operators can give references very quickly.

German Tactics

a. General

No-strict pattern is apparent in German operations. The Germans have in most instances employed a balanced and highly coordinated team of all arms and services, whatever the size of the force. Although their procedure has thus been elastic to suit the tactical situation, they have been found to proceed in general along the following lines.

b. Effect of Terrain

The Germans make full use of the freedom of maneuver which desert terrain affords and generally have not accepted battle under unfavorable conditions. Maximum use is made of the artillery and all auxiliary arms, both ground and air.

The lack of terrain obstacles and the supply difficulties have resulted in a modification of the German use of armored units in the desert as compared with their previous use in Poland and in Western Europe. In Libya, with the exception of isolated fortified localities such as Tobruk and Halfaya, no long defensive lines exist which can be probed to find a weak spot for penetration and exploitation. Nevertheless the cardinal principle of concentrating tank strength has been followed. On those occasions when the German forces advanced in several columns, the tanks were usually concentrated in one column. The object of the tank column is to destroy the enemy force, using maneuver to defeat him in detail whenever possible.

c. Formations

Various methods of advance have been used by German armored units. Usually the formation is in considerable depth. A battalion (65 to 80 tanks) frequently uses a "V" formation with two companies leading and one in reserve, or an inverted "V" with one company leading and two in reserve. Companies are usually in line, with tanks in column of threes at about 50-yard intervals and three to five tank lengths in depth.

A German tank battalion in tactical formation moves in short rushes, taking advantage of the terrain. Frequently the whole regiment advances in mass formation with lines of tanks at regular intervals of about 50 yards, advancing in waves. The relatively close formation is more readily controlled than a widely dispersed one. Field artillery and antitank weapons are kept up close, although their location is not apparent until they go into action, usually on the flanks of the tank column. The Germans have in the past been able to bring effective artillery and antitank fire to bear on the British before the British could effectively fire upon them. In addition, RAF planes, because of the pilots' inability to distinguish between their own and German tanks, have not attacked German tank formations in the forward areas.

d. Offensive Tactics

In the desert frontal attacks have not often been used, an effort being made more often to attack from one or both flanks. German tanks usually open fire at 1,500 to 2,000 yards, which is beyond the effective range of the hostile weapons that they have thus far encountered. When contact is made, the speed of advance is slowed down unless the movement is a quick thrust to force the withdrawal of weaker hostile forces. The 75-mm and 50-mm guns are used to keep hostile tanks out of range.

(1) Usual German objectives.— The object of the Germans is to knock out quickly as many of the antitank guns and foremost field guns as may be visible. When the German tank commander has decided to attack a position, his first objective has often been the British 25-pounders. By reconnaissance in tanks he first locates the British battery positions and makes his plans. This plan in principle always appears to be the same. He decides which battery to attack and he arranges to attack it from enfilade. His attack is made with 105-mm guns, the 88-mm dual-purpose guns, and both Mark III and IV tanks. The 105-mm guns fire from covered positions; their observation posts are in tanks. The 88-mm dual-purpose guns are towed. These guns use direct fire from their trailers after attaining defiladed positions at ranges varying from 2,000 to 2,500 yards. The Mark IV tanks assume positions in defilade and fire over open sights at ranges varying from 2,000 to 2,500 yards. The high velocity 75-mm gun in the Mark IV tank and the 88-mm dual-purpose gun have far higher muzzle velocities than any artillery that the British have had in the desert.

(2) German Mark III tanks.— The Mark III tank is used as the main striking force in attack. It has the dominant role in tank-versus-tank combat. Its heavy armor and powerful 50-mm gun give it a decided advantage over all types of tanks which it has thus far encountered in the desert. The 75-mm gun in the Mark IV tank is not an antitank gun but a close-support weapon. Its maximum range is 7,000 yards. Frequently these tanks use direct laying from a defiladed position in which, owing to the location of the gun in the turret, they offer a very small target. At other times the fire is massed, with indirect laying, and is adjusted by forward or flank observers in tanks. Tanks rarely

fire while moving, although in at least one instance they were used to fire a rolling barrage at from 3,000 to 4,000 yards while advancing slowly. This forced the opposing tanks to close up doors and turrets.

The first wave of Mark III tanks overrun the gun positions. The second wave of Mark III tanks is closely followed by the motorized infantry, which detrucks only when forced to and cleans up the position with small-arms fire, assisted by tanks which accompany it. After the artillery has neutralized the tanks, the support infantry is attacked. Such attacks have nearly always neutralized the artillery, either by destroying it when the attack was driven home, or by forcing it to withdraw before the tank attack was launched. A successful defense against such attacks has been made only when a tank force was available to launch a counterattack from concealed positions against the flank of the German tank attack.

(3) The German Mark IV tanks used as artillery.— In the attack the Germans maneuver to some position where their Mark IV tanks[15] can take up a position in defilade. The Germans meanwhile make a reconnaissance, probing the enemy from all directions to test his strength, and to induce the defenders to disclose their positions by opening fire. During this period, observation posts keep close watch, and any guns which disclose their positions are marked down for destruction when the main attack begins. Then, from their defiladed positions, the Mark IV's attack by fire all antitank guns or light artillery which are visible and within range. Light artillery, antitank guns, and machine guns with the same mission are pushed forward among and to the

---

15 The German Mark IV tank weighs 22 tons and carries 5 men. It has a maximum speed of 31 mph and is armed with one 75-mm gun and two light machine guns. Recent reports indicate that the Germans are modifying the design of this tank by fitting it with an improved 75-mm (2.95-inch) gun known as the "Kw. 40" and by adding hollow frontal armor. The Mark IV has hitherto been equipped with a low velocity 75-mm gun, and the tendency has therefore been to employ this tank as a close-support weapon. As a consequence of the mounting of an antitank gun--and the possible fitting of hollow frontal armor--it is to be expected that the Mark IV will in the future be, and may already have been, more boldly employed as a striking force in tank-versus-tank engagements. The German designation of this new equipment is Sturmgeschütz lange 7.5-cm Kanone (Stu. G. lg. 7.5-cm K).

flanks of the tanks. Observers and occasionally infantry are pushed further forward.

Each German tank battalion has one company of 10 Mark IV tanks, which are employed in 2 principal roles: as highly mobile artillery, and as a component of a fast-moving column. Often field artillery cannot be immediately available in armored engagements; the Mark IV tank with its 75-mm gun together with the artillery of the armored division provides German armored formations with the necessary heavy fire power for a breakthrough.

The maximum range of the 75-mm gun is reported to be 9,000 yards. This relatively long range dictates to troops equipped with light antitank guns the time and place of a battle. In addition, the speed of the Mark IV tank is sufficient to enable it to take part in a rapid advance with the Mark III tanks. The Germans have used these tanks as sniper guns, as artillery against forward British columns, and as heavy concealed weapons in the ambushes into which German armored cars have tried to draw the British cars. In a defensive situation the Mark IV is able to engage British troops from outside the range of the antitank guns, avoiding at the same time, by their mobility, the British artillery fire.

(4) Field artillery support.— The 105-mm mobile batteries and the 75-mm guns of the Mark IV tank furnish the principal artillery support for the German Mark III tank, which is the main attacking tank. Sometimes the 88-mm dual-purpose gun is used in conjunction with the Mark III tank.

Some reports indicate that the direction of this supporting fire is carried out by a system of air bursts, since air bursts have been immediately followed by HE concentrations. The fire of 75-mm and 105-mm guns using HE shells has not been reported to be extremely effective. Casualties caused to personnel and tanks by these weapons have been reported to be the result of a new flare—a 75-mm shell which envelopes the tank in flames regardless of what portion of the tank is hit. One whole tank regiment was reported destroyed by this type of projectile. Although the casualties caused from these weapons may be slight, all reports agree that they have a high nuisance value to tanks because of the blinding effect of the smoke and dust. The 88-mm is effective; tanks hit squarely by this gun are destroyed.

The Germans stress the use of ricochet artillery fire against personnel as follows:

> The much greater effect of ricocheting projectiles as compared with those bursting on impact has been confirmed by the testimony of numerous prisoners.[16] Against all living targets not covered from above, more ricochet fire than hitherto will be employed therefore. Ricochet fire may also be employed against concealed targets if it can be observed from the burst, the noise of the explosion, or the flash of the exploding shell that a sufficient number (40 to 50 percent) of ricochets, are occurring. Ricochets can be distinguished from projectiles which enter the ground by their sharper detonation sound, and by the brighter flash, visible even in daytime. This is particularly the case with shallow ricochets, which are easily mistaken for impact detonations. Projectiles which penetrate the ground make no, or very little, report and flash on exploding.

e. German Method of Forcing Gaps through Mine Fields

A heavy artillery concentration is placed on the point to be forced and upon the defending troops in the vicinity. After the defenders' resistance is lowered by the concentration, a comparatively small number of foot troops advance to the gap under cover of smoke or of dust raised by the concentration; they locate the mines by prodding the ground with bayonets or with mine detectors; the mines are then removed. Casualties are replaced from a reserve unit that is held immediately in rear. This method was used in

---

16 The use of slit trenches is universal among all forces in the desert.

forcing a gap through the mine field that was part of the defenses of Tobruk; the preliminary concentration lasted for two hours. After a gap is forced and marked, infantry followed by tanks or tanks followed by infantry attack through the gap. Infantry preceded the tanks in the battle of Tobruk.

f. Defensive Tactics

When an armored force is encountered, all tanks may take up a firing position in defilade, immediately reinforced by towed and self-propelled antitank guns and artillery. If the tanks are forced to retire, they withdraw under cover of antitank weapons and artillery. Usually the Mark III tanks withdraw first, the Mark IV assisting in covering the withdrawal with high explosive and smoke. When such withdrawals have been followed by the enemy, the well-concealed German antitank guns and artillery have caused such serious damage to the pursuing tanks that the pursuit has generally been stopped. Sometimes the tanks will withdraw through the antitank and artillery positions and then maneuver to strike the hostile armored force on its flank.

Antitank Operations

a. Organization

Since the number of guns in use in Cyrenaica has been inadequate, all available are used or emplaced before the close of each operation. The antitank weapons, which are considered artillery by the British, are under the command of the division artillery commander in the British forces, and he is responsible for so placing his artillery and antitank guns that they will be mutually supporting. For any action the artillery commander issues the necessary orders allotting the antitank weapons to both artillery and infantry units.

Antitank artillery regiments of 2-pounders consist of 3 battalions of 2 batteries of 8 guns each, totaling 48 guns. They are organized exactly in the same manner as the artillery units except for the number of personnel assigned. A few 6-pounder[17] and 18-pounder[18] batteries are being used. The 6-pounder guns are mounted portee, and the 18-pounders are truck-drawn. These units are also organized in the same fashion as the artillery batteries. The trucks used for the 2-pounders and 6-pounders portee are in general of the 1 1/2-ton type.

The minimum amount of antitank guns required with units necessarily depends on the type of country; the more open the country, the larger the number of guns needed. In the desert where there are no natural tank obstacles an attack may come from any direction. Headquarters and rear echelons must be protected. The large frontages covered and the wide dispersion necessary to minimize the effects of air attack make this problem of protecting rear elements a difficult one.

In the western desert there have been in use no antitank warning systems, but the British make use of armored car patrols to prevent any surprises, and, as a rule, when one weapon fires, all prepare for action. OP's to the front and flank warn by visual signals of the approach of enemy armor.

b. Positions

In some cases one battery of twelve 2-pounder antitank guns is detailed to protect each infantry regiment. Each attached supporting battery of artillery is often given one troop of four antitank 2-pounder guns. Organic artillery has the support of one antitank troop per artillery battery. These 2-pounder antitank units are not usually grouped or held in reserve at any point but are actually placed in positions from 100 to 300 yards from the unit protected.

British artillery regiments are armed with 25-pounders which, although not so designed, have formed the basis of the antitank defense. This has been necessary, because the 2-pounder antitank gun has not proved effective. The 25-pounders are sited to give

---

17 The 6-pounder is a new 57-mm. gun which is scheduled to replace the 2-pounder because of the latter's inadequate range.

18 The 18-pounder is an old type gun.

protection in depth, and, where the terrain permits, to give all-around protection to the position.

Antitank guns are placed to cover the 25-pounders in front, in intervals, and on the flanks. A proportion of them may have to be kept on wheels to counter a threat from an unexpected direction. The fewer the total number of antitank guns, the larger will be the proportion kept in mobile reserve. But positions which guns may have to occupy will in most cases be reconnoitered and prepared beforehand.

Despite the fact that the British have usually operated with one and sometimes two 48-gun antitank regiments to the division, they have still found the number to be too small, and consequently have had their choice of positions affected by the necessity of choosing terrain which could allow them the maximum use of their inadequate number of antitank guns. Unless otherwise dictated by the terrain, it is considered better to place the few antitank guns in comparatively small localities for all-around defense rather than to attempt a complete defense in depth over a wide area. The batteries of 25-pounders are used to provide depth to the defense. Antitank weapons are often placed from 100 to 300 yards on the flank of a battalion in action. For all-around defense of an organization, they are placed from 500 to 1,000 yards in front or on the flank of a battalion with instructions to move close to the battalion position when tanks approach within 1,000 yards of their positions.

c. Principles of Employment—German Tank Tactics

Since the antitank gunners have a formidable and important job to perform, knowledge of the enemy's capabilities makes it easier to accomplish. German tank crews are trained to try to gain the opportunity to register hits at 90° impact (i.e., get the target head-on or broadside). They attempt to put their own tank in such a position that it presents both front and side at an angle to opposing guns. Stationary firing is preferred, although they have fired on the move to force opposing tanks to close down, or to intimidate outposts and hostile gun crews. Artillery and antitank weapon crews have suffered many casualties from German machine-gun fire delivered from moving tanks. When antitank guns have held their fire until German tanks approached to within 600 yards, the crews have frequently been knocked out by machine-gun fire which penetrated their shields. If the ground permits, the German tanks move rapidly by bounds, firing between bounds when halted in hull-down positions.

d. Principles of Employment—British Tactics

All British antitank guns except 18-pounders (75-mm guns) are mounted portee on vehicles and equipped with ramps for unloading. These weapons have on occasion been fired from their vehicles.[19]

(1) Guns mounted on vehicles.—In using these weapons mounted portee, the gun is usually dismounted during firing, and the vehicles are removed under cover. The firing of guns mounted portee is unpopular, but when it is done, the vehicle is backed up to a point just below the reverse slope of a hill and the gun pushed up sufficiently to clear the crest. The driver of the truck must manipulate his truck on orders from the gunner in order to point the gun or place it in proper firing position.

Although firing guns mounted portee is frowned upon, reports indicate that some officers consider firing from portees to be necessary under the following conditions: (1) when on patrol with armored cars; (2) when on escort or convoy duty with supply echelons, headquarters, or brigade columns advancing across the desert to the attack. In such circumstances the object is to keep the enemy as far as possible from his prey and so enable the convoy to proceed without loss. Full use is made of the mobility of the portees, the opening range varying according to the thickness of the armor carried by the enemy raiding columns. Firing while the portee is in motion and opening fire on a moving target at over 1,500 yards or a

---

19 One observer reported that not a single case was known of dismounting an antitank gun during the period November 17 to 30, 1941, which was the intensive opening phase of the British 2d offensive. Firing portee has become increasing unpopular, however, and is no longer recommended.

standing target at over 2,000 yards are considered a waste of 2-pounder ammunition. Bren guns mounted on the portees are used to force the enemy to close down his hatches and so reduce his visibility.

Although the use of the antitank guns on portees is an improvisation, it has had some success. During the Italian retreat from Bengasi to Tripoli on February 6/7, 1941 the British sent three columns a distance of 150 miles in 30 hours to cut off the retreat. In the battle which resulted the antitank guns on improvised mounts encountered the Italian tanks, and 100 out of a total of 130 brand new M 13 Italian tanks were destroyed. One 1 1/2-ton truck carrying an antitank gun pointed to the rear went up and down the Italian column and claimed to have destroyed 25 tanks.

(2) *Direct laying at short range.*— Usually 2-pounder antitank batteries are directed not to use direct laying on tanks until the tanks are within 800 yards of their positions. For 25-pounders, direct fire is held until the enemy vehicles are within 1,000 yards. Opening fire at 600 yards has been found to be too short, because the enemy machine guns are then within effective range. At 800 yards the antitank gun is still comparatively as accurate as at 600 yards, whereas the machine gun has lost considerable accuracy and is likely to penetrate the gun shields. In one case near Sidi Omar in Libya, a battalion commander of 25-pounder guns, seeing a tank attack coming issued instructions for withholding fire until he gave the order. When the Axis tanks had approached to within 800 yards, commands for direct laying were given. The result was a bag of 10 tanks.

(3) *Guns placed well forward.*— All artillery and antitank weapons are placed well forward in either defensive or offensive situations. This permits the guns not only to support the infantry but to break up the leading wave of German medium (Mark III) tanks. In battle, 18-pounders go into action on the flanks of the battle position and well forward. These 18-pounder antitank

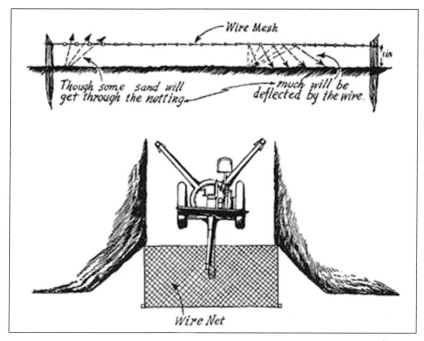

Figure 23.—Antitank gun emplacement

guns are truck-drawn and are of course kept mobile during an advance. All are fully manned and placed in position ready to fire when a halt is made.

The antitank guns are employed more often in pairs or bunches than as battalions or batteries. They are scattered about—often in pairs, and staggered, an effort being made to prevent a single strong sortie of enemy tanks knocking out all the guns. Positions taken are usually those which command a field of fire covering known danger areas. Wadis, large and small, are usually avenues of approach for hostile troops and are therefore given particular attention when siting guns.

(4) *Emplacements.*— Certain antitank guns have a very strong muzzle blast. In the desert terrain of the Middle East the force of this blast throws up a cloud of dust and sand that quickly reveals the position to enemy observers and often completely obscures the field of fire. Consequently, it is necessary to provide such guns with a blast screen. To eliminate this difficulty, a device is used which consists simply of a net of fine wire mesh,

supported on pegs extending about 1 inch above the surface of the ground. The wire mesh should be so painted as to blend into the surrounding terrain. Other provisions for eliminating the dust include covering the critical areas with concrete or cement, paving the areas with stone, or treating them with oil. These areas are camouflaged whenever the guns are not firing. Precautions are also taken to make the inside of the emplacements as dustproof as possible in order to prevent dust from being sucked up in the rush of air following the discharge.

Alternate positions are provided and all emplacements are constructed to permit easy removal of the guns. These provisions have been found indispensable, for the fire of the weapon will inevitably betray even a well constructed position.

When the terrain permits, the gun is defiladed from the enemy by emplacement on a reverse slope, or, if the country is flat, behind a natural or artificial mound. If an artificial mound is constructed, it should be as low as possible. The arc of fire is usually large; 180° is normal. The guns are given overhead camouflage where possible, but the coverings are constructed so that they can be easily removed when there is need to close station rapidly. Basically it is considered that the emplacement should be an open pit of minimum dimensions.

e. The Main Role: To Form a Secure Base

Every force, of whatever size, requires a secure base from which to attack if its intentions are offensive, or within which to maneuver for a counterstroke if its intentions are defensive. This problem is important in the desert where attacks can come from any direction.

On a large scale this secure base is called a "defensive position" by the British; on a small scale they termed it a "pivot of maneuver." The terms are really similar, the only difference being that the "defensive position" is made up of a number of "pivots of maneuvers."

The framework of the pivot of maneuver consists of the antitank gun positions, and the formation of this framework is the chief role of the artillery whether in attack or in defense. Every gun, field or antitank, is included in the framework. The framework also is strengthened temporarily by the inclusion of tanks in hull-down positions particularly in the case of a pivot of maneuver formed by an armored brigade. The field artillery performs a secondary role as well—that of producing bombarding or harassing or covering fire. The more exposed sites are allotted to the antitank guns. Every gun section has nearby infantry protection, the two forming together a definite defense area. The escort is armed with machine guns whenever possible.

(1) The Framework. —The actual form of framework, of course, varies with the ground. The main position is formed around the field artillery. Regiments are placed with their batteries in depth so that attacks from any direction will meet with an equal reception. A diamond formation often is considered the best solution. The positions of the guns are laid out so that the zones of fire interlock and at the same time so that the whole gun area can be covered with fire. Dead ground within the position is covered by antitank guns, normally drawn from those included in the composition of the field artillery regiments.

An outpost position in front of the main position toward the enemy is often required to prevent observation of the main positions. These outposts are formed of antitank guns, normally drawn from the infantry antitank companies, with the close escort of infantry, as mentioned above. The outpost dispositions are in depth, the front edge being placed on or just over the crest in front of the main position; and the antitank dispositions are coordinated with those of the main positions so that the whole area forms one complete net. The field artillery may be unable to carry out its secondary role (covering fire) if this outpost position is not provided.

A reserve of mobile antitank guns is held within the position. From this reserve, guns can be sent to give close support to batteries attacking from the "pivot," to extend the flanks of the outpost position if an enemy threat develops from an unexpected direction, or to strengthen the outpost line or the main position if the force is thrown temporarily on the defensive.

(2) In the attack.—The British consider that there are only two legitimate tasks for antitank guns in the attack; (a) to form the framework after a successful attack, and (b) to protect the flanks of attacking infantry tanks.

The antitank gun mounted on its portee is not a tank, and any attempt to use it as such by requiring it to accompany the leading waves of a tank or infantry attack inevitably results in severe losses. Every effort is made to place antitank guns in position at the objective as soon as it is captured.

The commander of the antitank guns detailed for consolidating the objective when captured is therefore given a free hand to move his guns as he thinks fit. Often it proves best to move the guns in bounds as the attack progresses. The antitank commander himself accompanies the commander of the unit that he is supporting, and on arrival at the objective makes a plan of the framework of the consolidation defense. If an enemy tank counterattack is launched before the consolidation framework is made, the antitank commander places his guns on or near the objective as soon as possible, and then uses them from the portees, taking advantage of any cover that can be found. Speed is essential, and it is for that reason only that he uses his guns as if they were tanks. If the consolidation framework has time to get into position, its object is to destroy counterattacking tanks. In this case, therefore, the antitank guns are used on the ground, concealed to the utmost, and dug in as thoroughly as time will permit. They are taught not to reveal their positions prematurely by opening fire at long range. Their fire is held until the enemy tanks are within the range[20] at which their armor will be pierced by the 2-pounder. Nearby infantry protection is provided with the guns, and snipers are placed to

---

20 800 yards against Mark III, 500 yards against Mark IV.

pick off enemy forward artillery observers who push in close with the object of spotting the antitank guns.

In protecting the flanks of attacking tanks or infantry, the object of the antitank artillery is to keep the enemy at a distance. Then the gun is used from its portee and opens fire at longer ranges. But since it is seldom possible to forecast the direction of an enemy attack, the guns are not normally committed to any positions at the outset. The antitank commander therefore keeps his guns mobile, and, together with representatives of his sub-units, carries out continuous reconnaissance of the area for which he is responsible, noting especially any ground in which hull-down positions are available: If an enemy flank attack develops, he moves his guns to meet it, either dropping into position on the ground to lie in wait when the enemy has to pass a defile, or fighting portee and using his mobility to prevent the enemy from closing the range.

(3) In the defense.—In the defense, the antitank gun has one object—to kill tanks. The enemy will, of course, do all that he can to spot and knock out the guns of a defense before he launches his tanks. Every effort is made, therefore, to prevent the positions from being disclosed until the enemy tanks advance to the attack and are within range of the antitank guns. The range must be short enough to enable the shell to pierce the armor. Harassing and bombardment tasks are carried out by the 25-pounder guns that are situated in covered positions.

The efforts to avoid observation are directed toward concealment and protection. Scrub ground, or other rough ground, is chosen wherever possible, and digging is done with great care. Movement of all personnel is rigidly controlled.

Guns are placed so as to give effect to the principle of concentration of fire. This is necessary, as the German tanks usually attack in a mass, which cannot be engaged effectively by single guns.

Guns are, therefore, normally sited by troops. The four

guns of the 2-pounder troop are spread over an area of about 400 yards square, and they must, of course, be mutually supporting. The four guns of the 25-pounder troops also adopt this formation if employed in a purely antitank role; but if the troop has a secondary role (covering fire) as well, it adopts a more concentrated formation in order to obtain fire control. For this purpose an arrangement roughly the shape of a half-moon, with intervals of about 70 yards between guns, has been found satisfactory. Depth within the field artillery regiment is obtained by siting the troops in diamond formation, 800 yards between troops, all troops being mutually supporting.

f. Effect of Artillery on Tanks

The following is the German teaching on the effect of field artillery on the tanks which they have encountered in the desert:

Armor of 60-mm or less is penetrated at ranges up to 600 meters by the 105-mm gun-howitzer 18 with angle of impact from normal to 30° using charge 5 or 6. The 105-mm gun, model 18, penetrates all thicknesses of armor encountered at ranges up to 1,500 meters with medium charge and armor-piercing shell. Direct hits from the 150-mm howitzer, model 18, with HE percussion fuze (instantaneous) projectiles have set enemy tanks on fire, or put them out of action by destruction of the drive mechanism. Thus, when engaging tanks with the heavy field howitzer, the bursts should not be largely over as when firing armor-piercing shells, but should be evenly distributed, some over, some short. Concentrations of artillery fire have been very effective against tank assembly points.

Smoke

Smoke, although not used extensively, has been employed occasionally in Libyan operations, and in these smoke operations the artillery has been one method of releasing smoke.

Conditions naturally vary, but observers report that smoke can often be used effectively. Some difficulties with the use of smoke are caused by desert winds, which are sometimes quite variable. Different sizes of whirlwinds which veer and change direction constantly make it difficult to estimate the wind when laying a smoke screen. Smoke has, however, many possibilities in connection with operations by armored formations.

a. Characteristics

Three main factors affect the use of smoke in the desert as elsewhere:

(1) The force and direction of the wind.
(2) Turbulence (which is the gustiness of the wind) and the effect of the bright sun on air currents.
(3) Humidity.

These factors do not remain constant, the force and direction of the wind being particularly liable to sudden change. Moreover, air eddies caused by the configuration of the ground may make the force and direction of the wind different at the spot where shells land and at the gun position. It is therefore impossible to specify particular weather conditions in which smoke will be effective. A decision on this point is reached usually by a method of trial and error, for which time must be allowed.

In desert areas high-explosive shell produces a substantial cloud of dust, and it may therefore often be practical to mix HE with smoke and so produce a satisfactory screen when conditions are not entirely suitable for the use of smoke alone. This fact also makes it possible to economize in the use of smoke shell and bombs, only limited quantities of which are usually carried.

b. Tactical Employment

All antitank guns depend on direct observation to obtain fire effect. If they can be deprived of their observation, their fire is automatically neutralized. In this fact lies the greatest value of smoke, particularly to armored divisions.

In attacks smoke has been used for the following purposes:
(1) To conceal local preparatory moves by supporting weapons such as antitank guns, machine guns, and mortars.
(2) To screen a forward movement preparatory to assault.

(3) To screen tanks from the observation of antitank guns and artillery observation posts on the flanks of the attack.
(4) To provide a smoke barrage on the front of the attack.
(5) To indicate the objectives to tanks.

Smoke screens required during the preparatory stages of the attack and during the advance to the objective are usually provided by the artillery. Assistance is sometimes given by infantry mortars when other tasks and the range permit. For a smoke barrage on the front of the attack, a crossing wind is necessary, and particular attention is paid to timing to insure that the attacking tanks are not placed in the dilemma of having either to wait for the barrage to lift, or to pass through it with the risk of being silhouetted against it on the far side.

In any attack some guns are either not located or not destroyed. In such situations some advantage has been obtained by smoke clouds laid down over the whole area,[21] for the lack of visibility usually hampers the guns more than the tanks. This smoke is not used to form a screen, for it is considered more effective to form a pall of smoke over the enemy defensive area.

In defense situations smoke is used to blind attacking enemy tanks. When used for this purpose, a smoke screen is put down beyond the effective antitank range. Otherwise it will merely assist the enemy by depriving the antitank guns of essential observation. The provision of a smoke screen of this kind usually is a task for the artillery.

German tanks in a hull-down position at over 2,000 yards' range are not only difficult targets, but also beyond the effective range of antitank guns. Much of the Axis fire is by direct laying. In many cases, therefore, the best method of dealing with Axis fire has been by a smoke screen. Care is then taken that this smoke screen is well clear of the British front lines, for if it is too close, it will merely serve as cover for the German advance.

While the smoke is in place, Axis unarmored troops are

---

21 Neutralization by high explosive is used, of course, when the approximate positions of these guns are known.

attacked by fire. Observation posts well out to a flank are found to be necessary, and every opportunity is taken to disorganize and cause casualties to the enemy while he is assembling for the attack.

Another use of smoke in the defense has been the blinding of the enemy's close-support tanks and other supporting weapons by interposing a smoke screen between them and the enemy assault tanks. This task may be within the power of both the defenders' close-support tanks and artillery. When smoke was used for this purpose care was taken to avoid assisting the enemy by providing him with cover behind which he could move forward infantry detachments in support of his assaulting tanks.

For covering a disengagment or a withdrawal, all types of smoke-producing weapons are used, smoke screens at the longer ranges being put down by the artillery, medium range screens by close-support tanks, and short range screens by the use of special dischargers and 2-inch bomb throwers. Tanks capable of producing tail smoke have also been used effectively for this purpose by both the Germans and the British.

Supply Methods

The outstanding characteristic of supply in the desert is the vulnerability of supply lines caused in large part by the fluidity of operations. The British have relied on supply dumps to a greater extent than the Germans, who use supply trains. The artillery plays an important role in the defense of both dumps and columns.

Supply trains are close up to maintain the momentum of the attack by supplying fuel and ammunition as required. Recovery crews go into battle with their units.

The Germans usually advance to the line of departure under cover of darkness in the early morning hours. They may give battle early in the morning, pause about midday for refueling and maintenance, and give battle again before dark. Return to bivouac is made after dark; hence the location of his bivouac area is difficult to discover. Whenever possible, tank attacks are made with the sun low behind the German tanks. Movement in the advance is fast—at least 20 miles per hour. The normal distance between halts, if no combat occurs, is about 40 miles. Refueling, replenishing of ammunition, and maintenance are carried out under the protection of artillery, antitank weapons, infantry, and overhead fighter protection. These operations are accomplished in full view of the enemy.

NEW GERMAN HEAVY ARTILLERY

Tactical and Technical Trends, No. 10, Oct. 22, 1942.

Indications that the Germans have recently introduced two new specialized heavy artillery weapons are found in photographs and captions appearing in a recent number of the German magazine Signal. The two accompanying sketches have been prepared from these photographs.

a. Heavy Mortar

The mortar piece labelled "Thor" is stated in the caption to have been used in the Sevastopol siege operations. Other photographs appearing in the same number of the magazine depict this mortar mounted on a caterpillar tractor, from which it is being fired. An

examination of this photograph by U.S. artillery and ordnance officers resulted in a consensus of opinion that the caliber of this mortar was probably between 500-mm and 600-mm. It will be remembered that at the time of the Sevastopol siege, both the German and neutral European press printed stories that the Germans were employing successfully a mortar of 560-mm caliber.

The development of a weapon of this type is to be ascribed to the ever-growing difficulties the Germans are encountering in mastering the Russian permanent fortifications. Forts and pillboxes are becoming stronger and stronger with the passing of each month; in consequence the attacking force is being required to use ever more powerful weapons of offense.

The mortar pictured has evidently a very short range, certainly not over 5,000 yards and possibly much less. In consequence, its usefulness is very limited.

Nevertheless, so important a role are modern fortifications playing in the fighting now raging in Russia, notably at Stalingrad, that it would appear probable that, as the war continues to develop, all armies, including our own, will find a need for artillery mortars of this approximate type in order to cope with the problem of destroying permanent land fortifications.

b. Railway Gun

The other type of German weapon portrayed in Signal is a very powerful railway gun. The caption in Signal suggests that this gun is mounted along the French Channel Coast. The question of the caliber of this weapon presents some difficulties. Photographs of the shell appearing elsewhere in Signal indicate, however, that it is at least of 16-inch caliber, but more probably between 20 and 22 inches. It is quite possible that this is the same weapon which has been reported on by British sources as follows:

"It has been established that 61.5-cm howitzers, probably on rail mountings, were used at Sevastopol. This weapon is reported to have 112 grooves in the rifling, and to fire a base-fuzed 'anticoncrete' shell (Betongranate) which weighs about 4,400 lbs, is 6 ft 9 in long, and has a copper driving band 2.76 in wide."

The range of this gun is not known, but is doubtless very great. The German purpose in mounting such a gun in France is not at all clear. It would seem quite possible that it is primarily intended for the bombardment of London and other inland British cities rather than for fire against channel shipping.

NEW GERMAN 105-MM GUN-HOWITZER

Tactical and Technical Trends, No. 30, July 29, 1943.

The standard German light field artillery piece is the 105-mm gun-howitzer, generally similar in appearance to the U.S. 105. It weighs about 5 1/2 tons, fires a projectile weighing about 32 pounds, and has a maximum range of about 11,000 yards. The German designation for this gun is "10.5-cm L.F.H. 18."[22] A few months ago, however, what appears to be a modification of this weapon was captured in Africa; it is believed to be the "10.5-cm L.F.H. 42." The "42" may also exist as a self-propelled gun; if so it is the first German field artillery piece so mounted.

In external appearance the most apparent difference in the two guns is the muzzle brake on the "42", a feature not known to be included in the "18", though it has been reported that there is an "18" with a muzzle brake which may possibly be designated "10.5-cm L.F.H. 18M."[23] The muzzle brake is of the standard double-baffle type, quite similar to the muzzle brake on the 50-mm antitank gun.

While the wheels of the "18" are made of a light alloy (current models may be of wood) the "42" has wheels at least partially constructed of wood; both types are rimmed with solid rubber tires as is usual in German artillery guns.

The main differences between the "18" and "42" are as follows:

	10.5-cm L.F.H. 18	10.5-cm L.F.H. 42
Length of gun (including breech ring)	106.8 in	117.75 in
Length of gun (including breech ring and muzzle brake)		130.87 in
Length of barrel	97.1 in	108.5 in
Length of bore	94.2 in	95.62 in
Length of chamber	8.35 in	12.87 in
Twist of rifling	Increasing 6° to 12°	Not Available

---

22 Leichte Feldhaubitze--light field howitzer

23 Abbreviation for Mundungbremse meaning "muzzle brake"

NEW GERMAN 105-MM GUN-HOWITZER (18M)

The "42" with its longer bore and chamber would appear to have a higher muzzle velocity than the "18." This seems to be borne out by the fact that captured "42's" are provided with a muzzle brake and have range table corrections painted on the shield of the gun. These tables, giving corrections for various charges, vary from minus 2 mils for an elevation of 100 mils to minus 70 mils for an elevation of 750 mils; presumably no range tables for the "42" exist or were available and it was necessary to use the "18" range tables with the above noted corrections to compensate for the greater muzzle velocity of the "42" gun. In addition to these necessary corrections it is also of interest to note that a special table for charge 6 (hollow charge ammunition) was also painted on the shield as follows:

Range (meters)	Elevation (Strich—mils)
400	7
600	11
700	14
800	16
900	19
1,000	22
1,100	24
1,200	27
1,300	30
1,400	33
1,500	36

THE EMPLOYMENT OF FIELD ARTILLERY

Military Intelligence Service, Special Series No. 8, December 20, 1942

The division artillery commander is a special advisor to the division commander on artillery employment, replacement, and ammunition; he is also commander of the artillery regiment, which includes the medium howitzer battalion, the sound-and-flash battalion, and such artillery as may be attached. He orders artillery concentrations, counterbattery, and harrassing fire in cooperation with the general scheme of maneuver and in support

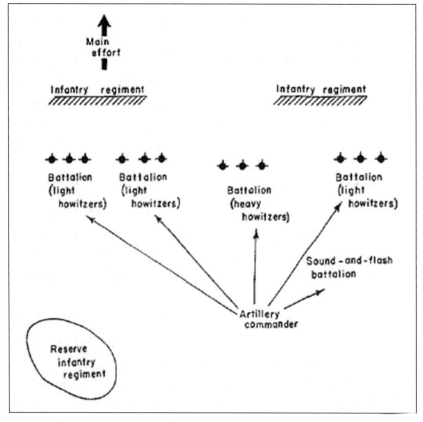

Figure 1. Artillery in a division attack.

of the infantry.

The artillery battalion is the fire unit. The battalion commander indicates definitely to his batteries such matters as the following: targets, aiming points, amounts of ammunition to be fired, time for opening fire, location of positions, ammunition supply, routes, types of fire, and kinds of ammunition. Firing data are obtained for the battalion by ranging shots, map computations, operations of the observation battalion (sound-and-flash), and references furnished by friendly troops. In very wide sectors or when operating in terrain of restricted visibility, it may be necessary for certain batteries to obtain firing data individually according to their tactical missions.

ORGANIZATION

Part of the artillery, usually the light howitzers, has the principal mission of providing direct support to the infantry. The remainder is employed in counterbattery, harassing fires and preparations, concentrations, and interdictions. Close connection with the sound-and-flash battalion is maintained. Disposition must be kept flexible to permit quick shifting of battery positions, missions, and targets. The employment in general is determined by these considerations: (a) number and kinds of guns available; (b) combat plans of the command as a whole; (c) terrain and weather; (d) hostile artillery; (e) ammunition available.

LOCATION IN THE ATTACK

In general, in the attack the artillery is located immediately in rear of the infantry line, just beyond range of hostile small-arms fire. Figure 1 shows a typical arrangement, with the observation battalion (sound-and-flash) operating directly under the artillery commander.

If reconnaissance and combat intelligence have given definite information about hostile dispositions, then a preparation may be fired, continuing 10 to 30 minutes, and depending upon the ammunition available, the surprise effect, and the situation. In the case where practically no information on the enemy is available, the artillery preparation is omitted; the infantry launches the attack, drawing fire from hostile heavy weapons and artillery, upon which, once located, the friendly artillery can thereafter fire.

LOCATION IN THE DEFENSE

Artillery in the defense is organized the same way as in the attack. The only difference in dispositions is that the direct support weapons (light howitzers) are located slightly farther to the rear, and the general support guns (medium howitzers) are in a central location where they can interdict at long ranges to force an early deployment of approaching enemy formations.

COOPERATION WITH INFANTRY

Time and space must be carefully coordinated by both the infantry and the artillery. It is essential that the artillery observers be at all times alert, not only to locate targets and hostile forces but to follow closely the movements of friendly troops, particularly the infantry. To facilitate this close contact, it devolves upon the infantry to seize and hold terrain which offers excellent observation for the artillery. Communication is effectively maintained. Close contact between infantry and artillery officers is absolutely essential. The division commander indicates, as promptly as possible, the plan of maneuver to the artillery commander so as to permit the latter the maximum freedom in planning the role for the artillery.

In the advance the artillery renders immediate support to the infantry when contact with the enemy is gained. This is accomplished by the artillery observers, who accompany the foremost infantry elements, or observe from balloon or airplane. In the attack the artillery must neutralize the hostile resistance and open the way for the advance of the infantry. Rapid reconnaissance and prompt deployment for action contribute to the success of this mission. It is generally advantageous for the infantry to wait for the support of the artillery. It is also important for the infantry to understand the limitations and capabilities of the artillery.[24]

---

24 In this connection: (1) the number, caliber, and effective range of batteries available; (2) the time necessary for preparation of fire; (3) the amount and kind of ammunition available; (4) the type of targets adapted to artillery fire.

ARTILLERY COMMAND IN THE GERMAN ARMY

Tactical and Technical Trends, No. 29, July 15, 1943.

In the German Army all artillery apart from the relatively small divisional allotment belongs to the GHQ pool (Heerestruppen). Units are allotted from this pool to army groups or armies according to the estimated needs. They may be sub-allotted to corps or divisions. The commander of the divisional artillery regiment, Artillerieführer or Arfü, commands the divisional artillery when it is not reinforced from the GHQ pool.

When GHQ artillery units are attached to the division, the Arfü is usually subordinated to an Artillery Commander, Artilleriekommandeur, abbreviated Arko, who with his staff is likewise from GHQ. An Arko may also be assigned to command an allotment of GHQ artillery to a corps. When no GHQ artillery has been assigned to an army group or army, an Artillery General Stabsoffizier der Artillerie, abbreviated Stoart, advises the army group or army commander on artillery matters. When GHQ artillery units have been attached to an army, a Higher Artillery Commander, Höherer Artilleriekommandeur, abbreviated Höh Arko, is assigned to the army. A recent report from British sources gives some interesting details as to the powers and duties of a Higher Artillery Commander of an army, and of an Artillery Commander.

a. Powers and Duties of a Higher Artillery Commander of an Army

The Higher Artillery Commander of an army is directly responsible to the army commander. He is at the disposal of the army commander for the supervision of the employment of artillery, for ground reconnaissance, and for any special tasks. He supervises artillery training within the army command and keeps an eye on the state of repair of artillery equipment. He is the commander of all army artillery directly under command of the army; as well as any of the army artillery units placed at the disposal of the Army High Command or the Army Group.

He has the right to attach himself to any unit within the army area, in which case he informs the appropriate headquarters. If he is not at army headquarters or in the immediate vicinity, an officer on his staff must be detached as liaison officer to the army headquarters. In any case, there is always close cooperation between the operational section of army headquarters and the staff of the Higher Artillery Commander.

The duties of the Higher Artillery Commander may be summarized as falling into 2 categories, namely, duties within the army area and duties within the army command. As regards all artillery within the army area his individual duties include:

(1) Organization of the employment of all methods for artillery reconnaissance, meteorological services, etc., in cooperation with neighboring armies;
(2) Control of artillery cooperation with the Air Force and with mapping and plotting units;
(3) The supervision of artillery training;
(4) Constant watch on the state of repair of artillery equipment;
(5) Participation in the delivery and return of guns;
(6) Submitting reports to the army high command as to experiences with artillery equipment;

As to army artillery within the army command his duties include:
(1) Assignment of officer personnel;
(2) Requests for, and distribution of, reinforcements;
(3) The control of supplies of weapons and equipment, clothing, motor transport, and tires.

b. Powers and Duties of an Artillery Commander

The Artillery Commander belongs to GHQ troops. He is assigned to a division or directly to a corps. He retains the right to attach himself to any artillery unit in agreement with the appropriate division headquarters. He maintains close cooperation with the higher artillery command of the army, and as regards signal matters has the cooperation of both divisions and corps signal battalions.

When under command of a division, he assumes the role of the Artillery Commander of the division. The division artillery is tactically under his command, but this need not alter its allocation to units.

As commander of corps artillery, or artillery group, he commands all artillery placed under command of the corps in accordance with the corps commander's orders. His duties include:

(1) Preparation for the employment of support artillery;
(2) Organization and use of support artillery;
(3) Fire-control of individual artillery groups;
(4) Cooperation of corps artillery with ground and air reconnaissance;
(5) Formation of an artillery signal net;
(6) Ammunition supplies.

In the corps area he is responsible for giving advice on all artillery matters, and for supervising artillery methods and training in the corps area. His duties include suggestions as to:

(1) Distribution of support artillery to divisions;
(2) Battle orders outside the division battle sectors;
(3) Tasks of artillery immediately under command of corps;
(4) Limits for counterbattery and harassing fire;
(5) Division artillery reconnaissance tasks outside the battle sectors;
(6) Regulation of artillery air services and reconnaissance;
(7) Regulation of artillery signal communications with the divisions;
(8) Provision of uniform plotting boards and range tables;
(9) Use of AA for protection of artillery;
(10) Ammunition supply.

RUSES FOR CONCEALING ARTILLERY POSITIONS

Intelligence Bulletin, July 1944

Some German artillery methods of countering Russian observation and sound ranging are analyzed in a recent article in the semiofficial Russian Army journal *Red Star*. Only those which are likely to be of interest to U.S. troops in the European theater are discussed here.

The Russians observe that since the results of sound ranging are dependent on atmospheric conditions, the Germans always try to exploit these. At times when sound carries the farthest—for example, at night, in fog, and when there is no wind—German artillerymen try to fire as little as possible. But when sound conditions are disturbed—that is, when there are head winds, vertical midday currents, sharp falls of temperature, and so on—their activity increases. The Germans also take sound into account when they are siting their guns. In Russia, this factor has led them to display a marked preference for reverse slopes, groves, lake shores, and marshes.

In Russia the Germans have used roving batteries extensively. These move around, firing a few rounds from each position—and occasionally undertaking more systematic fire. The Germans select positions which are a reasonable distance away from other friendly units. German batteries often are held in ambush, and for long periods do not fire at all. Almost never does a gun fire singly, lest this make it easier for Russian sound ranging to locate its position. Instead, it is a common German procedure for a number of batteries to fire together at an even tempo, so that all the sounds of gunfire merge.

The Germans have been using special devices to imitate the sound of gunfire. These have been placed from 200 to 300 yards to one flank of a well-camouflaged German battery, or some distance to the rear of the actual gun sites. Sometimes these devices are supplemented by others, which simulate muzzle flashes.

In line with this same principle, a German gun will register from a site 200 to 300 yards to one flank of its battery. If a gun were moved farther away, it would make the registration for the rest of the battery less accurate and, by getting out of the general area of the battery, would make the success of the ruse less likely. When the Germans are taking part in systematic fire, they wait until they believe that the opposition has located this gun. The Germans then open up with their remaining guns.

To give their muzzle flash a background against which it will not stand out, the Germans sometimes send up rockets or set haystacks on fire. Smokeless powder and flash reducers are also used. Sometimes German engineers erect dummy structures to conceal artillery pieces, as a camouflage measure against air and ground observers.

EMPLOYMENT OF GERMAN ANTIAIRCRAFT ARTILLERY AT SEVASTOPOL

Tactical and Technical Trends, No. 7, Sept. 10, 1942.

The account given below describes an interesting example of the employment of antiaircraft guns in the battle for Sevastopol. This article appeared in the German press in the middle of June, and shows clearly that 88-mm antiaircraft guns have been used against ground targets by the German troops in Russia just as they have been by the Afrika Korps of Field Marshal Rommel.

"The battle for Sevastopol is among the hardest of the war. Here the German Command was confronted with a narrow front barricaded completely with concrete, steel, and guns. But however heavy the barrage from the massed Soviet artillery, our antiaircraft guns succeeded in pushing through on several occasions and knocking out pillboxes at very short ranges so that our infantry could advance again. The initiative of the antiaircraft gun crews in the battle for Sevastopol was outstanding, and one particular instance has been singled out as an example.

"A lieutenant in charge of an antiaircraft combat detachment, who had been especially prominent in the fighting on the northern sector of the Sevastopol front, was ordered to support the infantry attack with one heavy gun and a light antiaircraft section, firing from a gully. The tasks of these antiaircraft combat detachments are almost always extraordinarily difficult. While the field artillery remains stationary for long periods in each position, the guns of the antiaircraft combat groups move close behind the first wave of the infantry, and engage over open sights and at very short ranges those pillboxes and other enemy centers of resistance which the infantry cannot overcome. Since the antiaircraft groups move normally without cover, they tend to draw the fire of all the enemy artillery. Such was the case here--and, in addition, the Soviet defenders had registered every yard of the ground.

"At first the task seemed impossible to the lieutenant. There was no field of fire for his gun from the gully, and the violent fire of the defenders made it impossible to advance. All alternative routes to the enemy pillboxes were also under heavy fire.

"Thereupon; the lieutenant decided on a bold gamble. Despite the intensive Soviet fire, he rushed his gun to a suitable position and opened fire immediately. By constant change of position and by taking cover momentarily when things became too hot, he was able to maintain an almost continuous rate of fire against his targets. In this way he succeeded in knocking out six pillboxes and, in conjunction with the light antiaircraft section, silenced a number of field works, machine-gun nests, and gun positions.

"Similar antiaircraft combat groups were employed on a number of other sectors. In practically every instance they are the first heavy weapons to follow the infantry. Although the way is first cleared for them by the engineers, it nevertheless requires skill and coolness to take the gun through the narrow gap in the minefields, where the slightest deviation may bring disaster. Furthermore the terrain at Sevastopol is extremely difficult. The long hillsides are covered with thick undergrowth and bushes, and bristle with pillboxes and weapon-pits. Concealed Russian snipers will permit the antiaircraft elements to pass unmolested and then ambush the supporting units as they come up. The German infantry, following its own artillery screen on a front of a few hundred yards, is subjected to continuous Soviet attacks, supported by artillery, from the flank. In these circumstances the situation has often been saved solely by the initiative of the antiaircraft combat groups and by the high rate of fire of their guns."

COMMENT: The above account appears to indicate that the Germans, at any rate at Sevastopol, used antiaircraft guns to give close support to the infantry. The high velocity and heavy shell of the 88-mm antiaircraft gun make it a formidable weapon against pillboxes and similar types of concrete defenses.

ARTILLERY IN COMBAT IN WOODED AREAS

*Tactical and Technical Trends,
No. 33, September 9, 1943.*

The following personal critique by a German artillery officer on artillery in combat in wooded areas is taken from a translated German document.

* * *

a. Example 1

An infantry regiment, reinforced by my light field-howitzer battery (probably 105's) horse-drawn, received orders, late in the afternoon, to push forward toward the east through extensive forest region, turn off to the right at a crossroad, and relieve the left flank of the neighboring division by making an attack.

It was nearly dark before the column of march advanced. The deep sand of the road and the necessary reconnaissance, caused the column to halt more than once. Tall trees alternated with those of recent growth. There were a few small clearings along the roadside but no large, completely cleared areas. The battalion to which the light field-howitzer battery was attached marched close behind the battalion forming the advance guard.

In the meantime, it had grown dark. The first shells burst over the point, more than a mile from the crossroad. Everyone halted and then the order rang out: "Antitank troops forward!" and "Artillery will fire!" The commander of the infantry regiment, who marched behind the point, turned to me and asked "Can you fire?" A fire mission! thought I. In a forest! At night! The enemy red-green map on a scale of 1:100,000! Our own position? The enemy? "Can you fire?"

One must try anything.

I hastened back and found a partially cleared place where one could fire fairly well between the trees. A gun commander was instructed to place at least one gun in position as quickly as possible. This took some time, for the infantry's moving of baggage and supply trains with the advance guard battalion barred the way of the guns. The din of battle grew ever stronger. While we were searching for gun positions, the gun commander asked me somewhat diffidently how he should lay and fire the gun with the map he had. I asked him in return, "Where is the most combat noise?" "There", he said. "Then aim your guns at that place! I estimate that the distance to our point is 800 yards. For safety's sake, begin to fire at 1,200, and fire two high bursts, then lower your gun and begin to use percussion fuzes. Bring your fire back to the target. Establish a forward observation post near the infantry."

"If things only go well," the expression on the lieutenant's face seemed to say.

And things did go well. We saw the third burst against the background of the evening sky. We fired shells equipped with percussion fuzes by ear (it had grown quite dark in the meantime) and brought the fire back to the target. The infantry was happy. It repulsed two attacks by the enemy.

We had not hit anything--the shots had gone over--and as the lines were only 30 yards in front of us, we couldn't bring the fire any closer. The infantry, however, swore by their artillery battalion, and the moral value of the fire, completely offset its lack of material effect.

b. Example 2

We, that is, our division and my light horse-drawn field howitzer battalion, relieved an armored division that had pressed forward to the western border of a strongly defended city but could get no farther because of deep minefields, tank traps, and the river. The period of position warfare lasted a month. We were at first provided with poor maps, but finally obtained captured maps on a scale of 1:50,000. The observation posts and command post were necessarily located at the edge of the wood 300 yards behind the front line. Only from the observation posts was it possible to get a fairly good view of the city and of the slowly rising open hinterland behind it. These posts were fitted up at night and carefully camouflaged. As we learned later from the enemy's position, these posts could not be seen. The flying bullets of the enemy infantry, however, constantly whined among the trees and made our stay there very unpleasant. The enemy artillery likewise beat the edge of the wood with a brisk fire. The fire-control wires were destroyed many times every day. Even the radio often failed us, largely because of the difficulty of supplying the anode batteries. The observation posts were connected with one another as well as with the battalion command post, and the battery positions were also connected with one another. Subdivisions of the battalion were interconnected; thus, for example, on a day when the enemy attacked and all the wires were destroyed by artillery fire, the fire of the entire battalion was controlled by the one remaining radio circuit of the battery within calling distance of the observation post.

c. Example 3

The enemy had pushed forward a salient in wooded and swampy terrain. The division, to which my mountain artillery battalion belonged at this time, was driven from the railway during the combat.

The infantry of both sides lay in the dense wood with lines not more than 50 yards apart. There were no elevated observation posts, consequently, our OPs were located in the front line. The longest view - 80 yards - was in a sparsely wooded area. In view of the dispersion, the center of impact of the barrage fire was 300 yards in front of the main line of resistance and consequently failed to accomplish its purpose. The fire was adjusted only by ear. It was necessary to adjust separately the fire of each of the guns laying the barrage and to check their adjustment separately twice a day. When our battery positions were surveyed in, we used map data to fire upon enemy positions, supply lines, and concentrations, deep within his combat zone (map on a scale of 1:50,000 and 1:25,000) and the fire was checked from time to time by aviators.

If the enemy was finally annihilated solely by artillery fire, this was due exclusively to the continuous bursts and harassing fire of the entire regiment. The expenditure of ammunition was heavy. My battalion (2 batteries) fired 17,500 shells during the 28 days. This method is really not "elegant", but it is impossible to do otherwise when fighting in wooded country.

d. Examples Compared

In example No. 1 there was no data relating to the position. The observation posts did not have a good view. Rough aiming in azimuth by ear, laying on any point, range estimated. In example No. 2 the positions were surveyed, the batteries interconnected, but only a small sector of terrain two miles deep could be seen from the observation posts. The laying was in the grid direction, ranges were obtained from the map. The regular firing method was used; smoke shells fired on a terrain, parts of which were not clearly visible. In example No. 3 the positions were surveyed but the observation posts did not have a good view. Laying was in grid direction, ranges obtained from map, fire brought back to the target by ear.

e. The Work in the Observation Post

In cases 1 and 3, the observation posts were located far forward. The lack of vision and the fact that the posts were located in the front line permitted the performance of only the most essential tasks. It was obviously impossible to employ the observation posts on a large scale. Radio, communication, supplemented by wire, and binoculars were the means used by the battery commander's representative. Corrections in azimuth and range, given in meters with respect to the line of sighting, were supplied to the battery. In case 3, the battery commander's representative was expressly forbidden to give ranges over the telephone or radio, as the interception service of the enemy was working well and could easily draw correct conclusions concerning the location of the battery positions from the ranges given.

In case 2, the fire was also affected by the "front-line influences", although an ordinary observation-post service could be maintained. Command posts A and B (instrument section) and the observation post, situated within call of its battery, were actually in communication because within calling distance. Moreover, it was possible to reach the other observation posts through the infantry command post; the battery positions could also be reached by means both of an infantry wire and that of an artillery group. The supplementary radio connections also permitted communication, but were less used, as the enemy located them by means of a radio direction-finder. The great importance of having as many lateral radio and telephone lines as possible was plainly indicated. The control of fire by the battalion was always assured. The observation posts in trees were occupied only in the most urgent cases. The observers, who wore safety belts, occupied positions in the forks of branches rather high up in the trees. One observation post could use the battery commander's telescope, but the others were restricted to binoculars.

With respect to camouflage, it should be mentioned that it is more important to have a good background, that is, trees with thick foliage, than to use camouflage on the side toward the enemy. The branches must be changed frequently and must be cut from trees of the same species.

f. Possibilities of Barrage Defense Against Enemy Attack

The event which causes the artilleryman the most pain is when a shell falls short and drops in his own lines. Artillery fire in forest combat reaches a decisive stage at just this point.

The barrage fire, whose center of impact was between 200 and 300 yards in front of our own front line, was adjusted by ear! No rule gives any information as to how the distance of detonations is to be estimated in a wood, without interrupting fire if possible, as in case 3. Nor can one decrease the range until the shells begin to fall in our own lines, when one learns that it would have been better to keep it at a distance. Moreover, sound is deceptive. Many bursts that sound far, away actually occur in the nearby underbrush, while many that sound near at hand result from detonation on distant trees. Here the difficulties begin.

Can we call fire directed behind the enemy's front line a barrage fire? In case 3, the enemy had always prepared for an attack in his front line, because he was safest from artillery fire there (according to the statements of prisoners). At most, the barrage blocks the second or third wave of attack and the supply lines. Our own infantry must always be apprised of this fact, for they must lay the barrage themselves.

Harassing fire and concentrations of fire on rear areas proved very effective, especially in case 3. This, in my opinion, is absolutely the only way in which artillery support can be useful in an engagement in the woods. If one has enough ammunition, the enemy can be driven out of the woods. There is little prospect, however, that artillery can be successful in supporting troops attacking in a forest. Enemy positions, supporting points, and bunkers can, at most, be recognized at a distance of 100 yards, a range at which the artillery can no longer fire upon them. Antitank guns, and particularly assault guns, on the contrary, have proven their usefulness. The forward artillery observer can at best only direct a scattering fire toward the rear. Attempts to measure the positions of tracer ammunition fired by forward observers have been useful in locating the position of the forward observer and the course of the front line. However, I would hardly recommend that fire be based on these measurements when all the tracer ammunition is not plainly recognized.

g. Conclusions

The lessons taught concerning artillery in a combat in the forest may therefore be summarized as follows:

(1) It is usually possible to fire only by ear in dense wood;
(2) The barrage as such is ineffective and constitutes a fire barrier

only in front of the rear areas;

(3) The artillery cannot support attacking troops, for it can fire only from clearings in the forest and areas containing scattered trees;

(4) The main value of artillery in a forest combat is in firing upon routes over which the enemy approaches and areas in which he assembles;

(5) It is suicide to observe from trees in a dense forest, owing to the proximity of the enemy's front line;

(6) As far as possible, only forward observers should be employed in a combat in the woods; to establish a larger "command mechanism" in the front line will cost many casualties;

(7) The nearer the front line and the denser the forest, the more facilities for communication should be established. It is sometimes impossible to find wires that have been cut by artillery fire in a dense wood;

(8) Interconnection is of value only when the observation posts have more or less view or no firing maps are available. It seems useless in a dense wood unless air observation is available for adjusting the fire. No liaison plane is needed when the target is shown on the map;

(9) Under certain circumstances, however, artillery should fire during an engagement in a forest even when its "material" ineffectiveness is obvious, for its "moral" effect is always obtained;

(10) The artilleryman must never forget to explain in detail to the infantry the artillery's role in a combat in the woods, so that the former will have no expectations that the latter cannot fulfill.

SIX-BARREL ROCKET WEAPON (THE NEBELWERFER 41)

Intelligence Bulletin, November 1943

I. INTRODUCTION

Whenever the fortunes of the German Army take a new turn for the worse, Nazi propagandists attempt to encourage the people of the Reich—and influence public opinion in neutral countries—by spreading rumors of new and formidable developments in German ordnance. Recently the Nazis have been releasing propaganda declaring that spectacular results are being achieved with the German six-barrel rocket projector known as the Nebelwerfer (smoke mortar) 41. Actually, this is not a particularly new weapon. Its name, moreover, is extremely misleading. In the first place, the Nebelwerfer 41 is not a mortar at all, and, in the second place, it can accommodate both gas-charged and high-explosive projectiles, as well as smoke projectiles.

It would be just as foolish to discount the German claims 100 percent as it would be to accept them unreservedly. Although fire from the Nebelwerfer 41 is relatively inaccurate, one of the weapon's chief assets appears to be the concussion effect of its high-explosive projectiles, which is considerable when the weapon's six barrels are fired successively, 1 second apart. The high-explosive round contains 5 pounds of explosive; this is comparable—in weight, at least—to the high-explosive round used in the U. S. 105-mm howitzer.

In view of the mass of misleading information which has been circulated regarding the Nebelwerfer 41—or, as the Germans sometimes call it, the Do-Gerät[25] —it is hoped that junior officers and enlisted men will find the following discussion both timely and profitable.

---

25 U.S. soldiers in Sicily promptly nicknamed the Nebelwerfer 41 the "Screaming Mimi."

Figure 1.—German Six-barrel Rocket Projector (side view).

2. DESCRIPTION

The Nebelwerfer 41 (see figs. 1 and 2) is a six-barreled (nonrotating) tubular projector, with barrels 3 to 3 1/2 feet long and 160 mm in diameter. The projector is mounted on a rubber-tired artillery chassis with a split trail.

There is no rifling; the projectiles are guided by three rails, each about 1/3-inch high, which run down the inside of the barrels. This reduces the caliber to approximately 150 mm.

The barrels are open-breeched, and the propellant is slow-burning black powder (14 pounds set behind the nose cap). This propellant generates gas through 26 jets set at an angle. As a result, the projectiles rotate and travel at an ever-increasing speed, starting with the rocket blast. The burster, which is in the rear two-sevenths of the projectile, has its own time fuze. The range is said to be about 7,760 yards.

The barrels are fired electrically, from a distance. They are never fired simultaneously, since the blast from six rockets at once undoubtedly would capsize the weapon. The order of fire is fixed at 1–4–6–2–3–5.

The sighting and elevating mechanisms are located on the

left-hand side of the barrels, immediately over the wheel, and are protected by a light-metal hinged box cover, which is raised when the weapon is to be used.

Each barrel has a metal hook at the breech to hold the projectile in place, and a sparking device to ignite the rocket charge. This sparker can be turned to one side to permit loading and then turned back so that the "spark jump" is directed to an electrical igniter placed in one of 24 rocket blast openings located on the projectile, about one-third of the way up from the base. About one-third of the length of the projectile extends below the breech of the weapon.

The projectile itself resembles a small torpedo—without propeller or tail fins. The base is flat, with slightly rounded edges. The rocket jets are located about one-third of the way up the

Figure 2.—German Six-barrel Rocket Projector (front view).

projectile from the base, and encircle the casing. The jets are at an angle with the axis of the projectile so as to impart rotation in flight, in "turbine" fashion.

The propelling cllarge is housed in the forward part of the rocket. A detonating fuze is located in the base of the projectile to detonate the high-explosive or smoke charge. In this way, on impact, the smoke or high explosive is set off above ground when the nose of the projectile penetrates the soil.

3. NOTE ON OPERATION

The following note on the operation of the Nebelwerfer 41 is reproduced from the German Army periodical Die Wehrmacht. It is believed to be substantially correct.

The Nebelwerfer 41, or Do-Gerät, is unlimbered and placed in position by its crew of four men. As soon as the protective coverings have been removed, the projector is ready to be aimed and loaded. The ammunition is attached to the right and to the left of the projector, within easy reach, and the shells are introduced two at a time, beginning with the lower barrels and continuing upward. Meanwhile, foxholes deep enough to conceal a man in standing position have been dug about 10 to 15 yards to the side and rear of the projector. The gunners remain in these foxholes while the weapon is being fired by electrical ignition. Within 10 seconds a battery can fire 36 projectiles. These make a droning pipe-organ sound as they leave the barrels, and, while in flight, leave a trail of smoke (see cover illustration). After a salvo has been fired, the crew quickly returns to its projectors and reloads them.

4. HOW THE GERMAN ARMY USES IT

The following statements have been made by a high-ranking German Army officer, and may be accepted as an authoritative expression of German ideas concerning the employment of this weapon.

Units of Nebeltruppen (smoke-laying troops) are organized as rocket-projector regiments (Werferregimenter), which are fully motorized and therefore extremely mobile. A rocket-projector regiment is divided into battalions and batteries, like those of the artillery. Since rocket-projector regiments are capable of playing a decisive part in battle, they may be concentrated at strategically important points along a front. ... The organization of a rocket-projector regiment is much like that of a motorized artillery regiment; organizationally, the motor vehicles and signal equipment of both are also much the same. Since the projector units usually are kept close behind the forward infantry line, their batteries may also be equipped with antitank guns. Because of the light construction of the projectors, a 3-ton prime mover is sufficient for traction purposes, and can also carry the gun crew and some of the ammunition. ...

The Nebelwerfer 41 can fire three different types of projectiles: high-explosive shells, incendiary projectiles, and smoke projectiles.

The high-explosive shells include those with supersensitive fuzes and those with delayed-action fuzes. The latter can penetrate reinforced cover. Because of their fragmentation and concussion effect, high-explosive shells are used primarily against personnel. It has been found that the concussion has not only been great enough to kill personnel, but occasionally has caused field fortifications and bunkers to collapse.

The incendiary projectiles are psychologically effective, and under favorable conditions can start field and forest fires.

The smoke projectiles are used to form smoke screens or smoke zones.

Rocket-projector troops are employed as battalion and regimental units, in keeping with their task of destroying hostile forces by concentrated fire. One of the advantages of the Nebelwerfer 41 is that it can mass its projectiles on a very small target area. By means of a shrewd disposition of the batteries, a carefully planned communication system, and a large number of observation posts with advanced observers, the infantry can assure for itself maneuverability and a concentration of its fire power upon the most important points. Projectors are placed well toward the front—almost without exception, at points forward of the artillery—so that they will be able to eliminate hostile command posts, destroy hostile positions, and even repulse sudden attacks effectively. The firing positions of the projectors are always carefully built up so that the weapons can give strong support to the infantry.

In Russia, during the winter of 1942-43, many breakthrough attempts by hostile forces were repulsed by direct fire from rocket-projector batteries.

TACTICAL EMPLOYMENT OF GERMAN 75-MM ASSAULT GUN

Tactical and Technical Trends, No. 19, February 25, 1943.

The German 75-mm assault gun (7.5-cm Sturmgeschütz) is a weapon comparable to the U.S. 75-mm and 105-mm self-propelled guns. The gun and mount weigh about 20 tons. Its maximum speed cross-country is about 7 mph, on roads about 22 mph; it can average about 15 mph. On normal roads its radius of action is about 100 miles, cross-country about 50 miles. To move an assault-gun battery 100 kilometers (about 65 miles) requires 4,000 liters (about 1,050 gallons) of gasoline. The range of the 75-mm short-barrelled tank gun (7.5-cm KwK), with which this weapon was originally equipped, is about 6,000 yards.

It is reported that there are now apparently three types of assault guns in service. These are: the Stu.G. 7.5-cm K, mounting the 7.5-cm KwK (short-barreled tank gun--23.5 calibers[26]); the Stu.G. lg. 7.5-cm K, mounting the 7.5-cm KwK 40 (long-barreled tank gun--43 calibers); and a third weapon, nomenclature at present unknown, which appears to have a 75-mm gun with a bore 30 calibers in length. It seems probable, therefore, that the 7.5-cm KwK 40, which is the principal armament of the new Pz. Kw. 4 (Mark IV tank), may be primarily an antitank weapon, while the latest intermediate gun will take the place of the old Stu.G. 7.5-cm K as a close-support weapon.

While some technical details of this weapon have been known for some time, relatively little information has been available until recently concerning its tactical employment. Two German documents on the tactical use of this weapon have now been received. One is dated May 1940, the other April 1942. The

---

26 Length of bore

second document is essentially identical in substance with the first, except that the second contains some additional information. Both documents have been combined into one for the present report, and such apparent contradictions as exist are noted in the translation which follows.

* * *

INSTRUCTIONS FOR THE EMPLOYMENT OF ASSAULT ARTILLERY

a. Basic Principles and Role

The assault gun (7.5-cm gun on an armored self-propelled mount) is an offensive weapon. It can fire only in the general direction in which the vehicle is pointing[27] Owing to its cross-country performance and its armor, it is able to follow anywhere its own infantry or armored troops.

Support for the infantry in attack is the chief mission of the assault gun by virtue of its armor, maneuverability, and cross-country performance and of the rapidity with which it can open fire. The moral support which the infantry receives through its presence is important.

It does not fire on the move. In close fighting it is vulnerable because its sides are light and it is open-topped. Besides, it has no facilities for defending itself at close quarters. As it is not in a position to carry out independent reconnaissance and fighting tasks, this weapon must always be supported by infantry.

In support of an infantry attack, the assault gun engages the enemy heavy infantry weapons which cannot be quickly or effectively destroyed by other weapons. In support of a tank attack, it takes over part of the role of the Pz. Kw. 4, and deals with enemy antitank guns appearing on the front. It will only infrequently be employed as divisional artillery, if the tactical and ammunition situation permits. Assault artillery is not to be included in the divisional artillery fire plan, but is to be treated

---

27 Traverse is limited to 20 degrees

only as supplementary, and to be used for special tasks (e.g., roving batteries). Its employment for its principal tasks must always be assured.

[The April 1942 document states that "The assault gun may be successfully used against armored vehicles, and light and medium tanks." The May 1940 document, however, states "It is not to be used for antitank purposes, and will only engage enemy tanks in self-defense or where the antitank guns cannot successfully deal with them." This apparent contradiction can perhaps be explained by the fact that, prior to the invasion of Russia in 1941, this weapon had been used in limited numbers only. Experience on the Eastern Front may have shown that it could be successfully used against tanks, although Russian sources refer to it as essentially an infantry support weapon. A more logical explanation perhaps lies in two German technical developments since 1940: namely, hollow-charge ammunition, which is designed to achieve good armor-piercing performance at relatively low muzzle velocities, and the reported replacement of the short-barreled low-velocity 75-mm with the long-barreled high-velocity tank gun (7.5-cm KwK 40) on some of the newer models.]

b. Organization of the Assault Artillery Battalion and Its Batteries

The assault gun battalion consists of battalion headquarters and three batteries. The battery has six guns--three platoons, each of two guns.[28] The command vehicles for battery and platoon commanders are armored. They make possible, therefore, movement right up to the foremost infantry line to direct the fire.

c. Principles for Employment

Assault gun battalions belong to GHQ artillery. For the conduct of certain engagements, battalions or separate batteries are attached to divisions, or to special task forces. The division commander

---

28 The April 1942 document states that a battery has 7 guns, the extra gun being "for the battery commander."

should attach some or all of the assault artillery batteries under his control to infantry or tank units; only in exceptional circumstances will they be put under the artillery commander. Transfer of batteries from support of one unit to another within the division can be carried out very quickly in the course of a battle. Close liaison with the batteries and within the batteries is of primary importance for the timely fulfillment of their missions. The assault artillery fires from positions in open ground, hidden as far as possible from ground and air observation. Only when employed as part of the divisional artillery will these guns fire from covered positions.

Splitting up of assault-gun units into small parts (platoons or single guns) jeopardizes the fire power and facilitates enemy defense. This should occur only in exceptional cases when the entire battalion cannot be employed, i.e., support of special assault troops or employment over terrain which does not permit observation. If employed singly, mutual fire support and mutual assistance in case of breakdowns and over rough country are not possible.

As complete a picture as possible must be obtained of the enemy's armor-piercing weapons and the positions of his mines; hasty employment without sufficient reconnaissance might well jeopardize the attack. Premature deployment must also be avoided. After an engagement, assault guns must not be given security missions, especially at night. They must be withdrawn for refuelling, overhauling, and resupply. After 4 to 5 days in action, they must be thoroughly serviced. If this is not possible, it must be expected that some will not be fit for action and may fall out. When in rear areas, they must be allotted space near repair shops so that they are readily accessible to maintenance facilities, etc.

Troops co-operating with assault guns must give all support possible in dealing with mines and other obstacles. Artillery and heavy infantry weapons must give support by engaging enemy armor-piercing weapons.

Surprise is essential for the succcssful employment of assault-gun battalions. It is therefore most important for them to move up and into firing positions under cover, and generally to commence fire without warning. Stationary batteries fire on targets which are for the moment most dangerous to the infantry (especially enemy heavy infantry weapons), destroy them, and then withdraw to cover in order to avoid enemy fire. With the allotment of smoke ammunition (23 percent of the total ammunition issue),[29] it is possible to lay smoke and to blind enemy weapons which, for example, are sited on the flank. Assault artillery renders support to tanks usually after the hostile position has been broken into. In this role, assault-gun batteries supplement Pz. Kw. 4s, and during the fluid stages of the battle direct their fire against enemy antitank weapons to the direct front. They follow very closely the first waves of tanks. Destruction of enemy antitank weapons on the flanks of an attack will frequently be the task of the Pz. Kw. 4.

Against concrete positions, assault guns should be used to engage casemates with armor-piercing shells. Co-operation with assault engineers using flame-throwers is very effective in these cases.

Assault guns are only to be used in towns and woods in conjunction with particularly strong and close infantry support, unless the visibility and field of fire are so limited as to make use of the guns impossible without endangering friendly troops. Assault guns are not suitable for use in darkness. Their use in snow is also restricted, as they must usually keep to available roads where enemy defense is sure to be met.

(a) On the Move

Vehicles on the move should be kept well spaced. Since the average speed of assault guns is about 15 mph, they must be used in leap-frog fashion when operating with an infantry division. Crossing bridges must be the subject of careful handling. Speed must be reduced to less than 5 mph, and the assault guns must keep exactly to the middle of the bridge, with intervals of at least 35 yards.

---

29 According to the April 1942 document, the issue is only 10 percent smoke. It is probable that the ammunition issue depends on the particular operations involved.

Bridges must be capable of a load of 22 tons. The commander of the assault guns must cooperate with the officer in charge of the bridge.

(1) In the Infantry Division

While on the move, the division commander keeps the assault-gun battalion as long as possible under his own control. According to the situation and the terrain he can, while on the move, place one assault gun battery in each combat team. The attachment of these weapons to the advance guard is exceptional. In general, assault gun batteries are concentrated in the interval between the advance guard and the main body, and are subject to the orders of the column commander.[30] On the march, the battery commander and his party should accompany the column commander.

(2) In the Armored Division

On the move, the assault gun battalion attached to an armored division can be used to best advantage if included in the advance guard.

(b) In the Attack with an Infantry Division

The division commander normally attaches assault-gun batteries to the infantry regiments. On receipt of orders placing him under command of an infantry regiment, the battery commander must report in person to the commander of that infantry regiment. Exhaustive discussion between these two (as to enemy situation, preparation of the regiment for the attack, proposed conduct of the attack, main point of the attack, co-operation with divisional artillery, etc.) will provide the basis for the ultimate employment of the assault-gun battery.

It is an error to allot to the battery tasks and targets which can be undertaken by the heavy infantry weapons or the divisional artillery. The battery should rather be employed to engage such nests of resistance as are not known before the beginning of the attack, and which, at the beginning or in the course of the battle,

---

30 The April 1942 document states that "an assault gun battery well forward in the advance guard may ensure the rapid crushing of enemy resistance." It does not specify whether this is applicable to operations with infantry or with armored elements.

cannot be quickly enough engaged by heavy infantry weapons and artillery. It is the special role of the assault-gun battery to assist the infantry in fighting its way through deep enemy defense zones. Therefore, it must not be committed until the divisional artillery and the heavy infantry weapons can no longer render adequate support.

The attached battery can be employed as follows:

(1) Before the attack begins, it is located so as to be capable of promptly supporting the regiment's main effort; (or)
(2) The battery is held in the rear, and is only committed if, after the attack begins, a clear picture is obtained of the enemy's dispositions.

Under both circumstances the attachment of the battery, and occasionally of individual platoons, to a battalion may be advantageous.

The commander under whose command the battery is placed gives the battery commander his orders. The latter makes clear to his platoon commanders the specific battle tasks, and shows them, as far as possible on the ground, the targets to be engaged. When in action the battery commander, together with his platoon commanders, must at all times be familiar with the hostile situation, and must reconnoiter the ground over which he is to move and attack. The battery will be so disposed by the platoon commanders in the sectors in which it is expected later to operate that, as it approaches the enemy, the battery, under cover, can follow the infantry from sector to sector. How distant an objective can be given, and yet permit the control of fire by the battery and platoon commanders, is dependent on the country, enemy strength, and enemy action. In close country, and when the enemy weapons are well camouflaged, targets cannot be given to the platoons by the battery commander. In these circumstances, fire control falls to the platoon commanders. The platoons must then co-operate constantly with the most advanced infantry platoons; they remain close to the infantry and engage the nearest targets. The question of dividing a platoon arises only if individual guns are allotted to infantry companies or platoons to carry out specific tasks: e.g., for action deep into the enemy's battle position.

In an attack by tanks attached to an infantry division, the assault-artillery battalion engages chiefly enemy antitank weapons. In this case too, the assault-gun battalion is attached to infantry elements. Well before the beginning of the tank attack, the batteries are disposed in positions of observation from which they can readily engage enemy antitank weapons. They follow up the tanks by platoons, and under special conditions--e.g., in unreconnoitered country-- by guns, as soon as possible. In a deep attack, co-operation with tanks leading an infantry attack is possible when the hostile islands of resistance have been disposed of.

In the enemy tank counterattack, our own antitank guns first engage the hostile tanks. The assault-gun battalion engages the enemy heavy weapons which are supporting the enemy tank counterattack. Only when the antitank guns prove insufficient, do assault guns engage enemy tanks. In this case the assault guns advance within effective range of the enemy tanks, halt, and destroy them with antitank shells.

(c) In the Attack with an Armored Division

In such an attack, the following tasks can be carried out by the assault gun battalion:

(1) Support of the tank attack by neutralizing enemy antitank weapons; (and/or)

(2) Support of the attack by motorized infantry elements.

According to the situation and the plan of attack, the battalion, complete or in part, is attached to the armored brigade, sometimes with parts attached also to the motorized infantry brigade. Within the armored brigade, further allotment to tank regiments is normally necessary. As a rule, complete batteries are attached.

To support the initial phase of the tank attack, assault-gun batteries can be placed in positions of observation if suitable ground is already in our possession. Otherwise the batteries follow in the attack close behind the first waves of tanks, and as soon as the enemy is engaged, support the tanks by attacking enemy antitank weapons.

As the tank attack progresses, it is most important to put enemy defensive weapons out of action as soon as possible. Close support of the leading tanks is the main essential to the carrying out of these tasks.

The support of the motorized infantry attack is carried out according to the principles for the support of the foot infantry attack.

(d) In the Attack as Divisional Artillery

In the attack of a division, the employment of the assault gun battalion as part of the divisional artillery is exceptional. In this role, the assault-gun batteries must be kept free for their more usual mission at all times, and must enter battle with a full issue of ammunition.

(e) In the Pursuit

In the pursuit, assault-gun batteries should be close to their own infantry in order to break at once any enemy resistance. Very close support of the leading infantry units increases their forward momentum. Temporary allotment of individual platoons—under exceptional circumstances, of individual guns—is possible.

(f) In the Defense

In the defense, the primary task of assault artillery is the support of counterthrusts and counterattacks. The assembly area must be sufficiently far from the friendly battle position to enable the assault-gun units to move speedily to that sector which is threatened with a breakthrough. Allotment and employment are carried out according to the plan of the infantry attack. The point of commitment should be arranged as early as possible with the commanders of the infantry units allocated to the counterthrust or counterattack. In the defense as in the attack, the assault-artillery battalion will only be employed in an antitank role if it must defend itself against a tank attack. (Only 12 percent of the ammunition issue is armor-piercing.)[31] If employed as part of the divisional artillery (which is rare), the battalion will be placed under the division artillery commander.

(g) In the Withdrawal

For the support of infantry in withdrawal, batteries, and even individual platoons or guns, are allotted to infantry units. By virtue of their armor, assault guns are able to engage enemy targets even when the infantry has already withdrawn. To assist disengagement from the enemy, tank attacks carried out with limited objectives can be supported by assault guns. Allotment of assault-gun batteries or platoons to rear parties or rear guards is effective.

d. Supplies

As GHQ troops, the battalion takes with it its complete initial issue of ammunition, fuel, and rations. When it is attached to a division, its further supply is handled by the division. The battalion commander is responsible for the correct supply of the battalion and the individual batteries, especially in the pursuit. Every battery, platoon, and gun commander must constantly have in mind the supply situation of his unit. It is his duty to report his needs in sufficient time and with foresight, and to take the necessary action to replenish depleted supplies of ammunition, fuel, and rations.

---

31 15 percent according to the April 1942 document.